BUTCHER, BITER, SPY

A TRUE STORY OF MADNESS, MUTILATION AND UNSPEAKABLE ACTS OF BRUTALITY

RYAN GREEN

For Helen, Harvey, Frankie and Dougie

Disclaimer

This book is about real people committing real crimes. The story has been constructed by facts but some of the scenes, dialogue and characters have been fictionalised.

Polite Note to the Reader

This book is written in British English except where fidelity to other languages or accents are appropriate. Some words and phrases may differ from US English.

ISBN: 979-8366639910

CONTENTS

Boom Town

Across the globe men, women, and children of every free nation rejoiced. The war was at an end. Surely that would be the end of all war. Nobody could conceive of unleashing such nightmares again. There was an entire generation for whom the faintest scent of turned soil or chlorine cleaner was enough to reduce them to quivering wrecks. Men who had been considered the bravest and the boldest of their kind cruelly haunted by the horror of it all.

Nobody would call them cowards. Nobody that had seen war's true face. Nobody that had heard the artillery howl. The whole world was united in their praise of those heroes who had looked the devil in the eye. It was a time of rejoicing, regrowth, glory.

Except here. Except in Germany.

Faced with an unwinnable war and allies dropping like flies, the German leadership had surrendered utterly. They had surrendered all of the gains that they had made, retreated behind old borders, and begged forgiveness from the rest of the world. They had taken on the mantle of the monster, the aggressor, the villain of the Great War, and now all who lived under their flag were paying the price for it.

Reparations, they had called it, when the grain houses and farms were looted. Reparations, when every penny in the banks was scraped out and handed over. Reparations, when Germany submitted and surrender ed and licked the boots of men who were not worthy to walk her soil.

There was no triumph here, no rejoicing. Only the agony of loss and the cold realisation that this was all that the future would hold. The republic, clawed from the ashes of what had been an empire in the making, was unsteady on its feet. A starved and desperate animal, wheezing its way along. Yet down on the streets, the common man was doing what common men have always done during times of hardship after fate or history dealt a crippling blow. They were surviving.

Day by day, they were living. Making the last of the flour stretch to another loaf. Digging in the back of pantries for the pickles that probably should have been long gone. Buying a sausage or two on the black market when the rations just wouldn't cover the whole week. Asking no questions, getting no lies.

And just like everywhere where the human spirit was ground down into the dirt, just like every people driven to the brink of destruction, the German people found hope and joy at the bottom of the barrel. They found music, and dancing. They found culture and love and acceptance among their kind.

The cabaret was born in this time of strife, all the outliers and oddities of society given centre stage, praised and adored for their strangeness, where the last generation would have cursed and decried them. A whole nation was realising that the world was not black and white as they had all been told, they were not the chosen people, they were not the heroes of the story, so what else had been a lie? All this time, everyone had struggled and strived to fit inside the little boxes that society demanded, and for what? This was their reward?

They could not fight the world. They could not fight the leaders that had brought them here. There was no one place that they could go and take a swing at somebody that would make a difference. So, this was their rebellion. As they starved, they sang. As their world tumbled down around them, they danced amidst the ruins.

What should have been a time of despair became a time of rebirth, most of all for the people who had lived their lives closeted and hidden from the light of day. There was a sexual revolution the likes of which the rest of the world would not see for half a century. And nowhere could this revolution be more clearly seen than in the cities.

All the vast factories that had been set to the task of producing munitions now lay silent. The jobs that had occupied every set of idle hands were now gone. While many fled the city for the dubious comforts of home, more people still flooded to the great cities of Germany. The ones who had never fit in, the ones who needed to make a new life for themselves, just as Germany needed new life injected into it. With merely the whisper of the nightlife as a lure, these people were drawn, like moths to a flame, into cities that should have been dead and gone.

There were fatherless sons aplenty in those days, boys that had lost their fathers to the war, as well as boys that had lost their fathers due to old-fashioned ideas about what a man should be. And it was to the cities that these boys all fled. To seek out not a better life, but one that they could live more honestly. They might have had to stand in line for bread, but when night fell the abandoned bomb factories lay quiet while the cabarets opened and allowed these young men to come alive, some of them for the first time in their lives.

But the thing about moths being drawn to a candle is that in the end, they get burned.

Fritz stood outside the train station in the middle of Hanover, hand -rolled cigarette dangling limp from his lip, arms crossed, hat pulled low. He'd look like nobody to anyone strolling by. Just waiting for a friend's train to arrive. He wasn't there to be seen; he was there to watch.

The vast majority of the people filtering out from the station were just the usual lot, men coming back from where the war had flung them to try and rebuild something like a life. Women that had gone out to identify the bodies of their sons and their husbands. They were sombre, heads down, eyes down. They didn't hold Fritz's interest. He was looking for something else.

There were the workers, moving from city to city, trying to find a factory that was still in operation, that had the raw materials to produce and the money to pay. More and more of them passed through every day. The hope on their faces was always tempered with the cold weight of reality, their eyes were down too. Like they thought they might scare off opportunities should they look them straight in the eye. Some of them, Fritz gave a second assessment. They wouldn't be the first to ride into this town under a false flag, scared of what might happen if they let their true colours show. In the end, however, they were older than he'd like and had been made strong from a lifetime of hard work. He had no more desire to tangle with them than with the veterans.

It was the last group, dotted throughout the mass of humanity like sprinkles on top of a sundae, that Fritz was looking for. The ones who came off the train with smiles on their faces, eyes up, taking it all in. Hope wasn't just an idea to them, it was something that they lived and breathed. They didn't have to lean on luck to get them to where they wanted to be in life because where they wanted to be was right here, right now. This was the distant dream that so many of them hadn't even known was a possibility. They were his people. They were his prey.

Today, there was a halfway decent crop of them, all coming out of the station in a knot. It seemed that they'd found one another, birds of a feather flocking together, even if those particular feathers ended up in boas. They'd bunched up, either while travelling or in the last city. Less than ideal. Fritz couldn't work a group. He needed one of them on their own. One that needed a helping hand, some guidance from an older and wiser elder of the scene. Somebody who would put them up and take care of them a little bit while they found their feet in a new, scary place.

At the tail end of the disembarking passengers, he spotted his mark. So clean -shaven he looked like a boy, eyes flitting about restlessly, but a nervous smile tugging at his lips too. He could have been thirteen and it wouldn't have surprised Fritz, he supposed the boy was probably older, maybe even eighteen, but the aesthetic of the thing was what mattered to him most. Not the numbers.

Picking the kid up was the easiest thing in the world now that he'd done it so many times. It was like reading off a script, everything he said, everything the boy said, back and forth with the predictability of the ticking of the clock overhead.

New in town, need someplace to stay, worry about it later, get a drink now, really need someplace to put your case down first, nothing to worry about, drop it at my place, live a little, first time in town, see the sights.

He could do it in his sleep. He could do it with one hand tied behind his back. With both hands behind his back. It was like he'd been born to do this. Like all his life, he'd just been waiting for the universe to catch up and provide him with this exact situation, looped over and over again.

In a bar that would become a cabaret once the sun was fully set, they drank gin and swapped stories. Fritz had heard them all before. The boy had heard none of them before, and he was laughing and laughing. His head was thrown back and his Adam's apple was bobbing up and down with each snort and giggle.

Fritz wet his lips, brought his glass back up to his face and took a dainty sip to keep the hunger in his expression from seeming too obvious. Being that it was still early, it was likely that some of those in attendance were not the sort of people you could depend on to look the other way should you do something a bit naughty. Fritz knew he had to be subtle enough that anything he might do would be overlooked or dismissed with little explanation. When he let his foot rest on the boy's calf under the table, it was casual enough that it might have been an accident. When he leaned in closer to hear what the boy was saying, it was because the place was loud, not because he was intoxicated by his proximity to another man. When he reached under the table to take the boy's hand and lead him out of the place, it wasn't because they were going to do anything so crass as to have sex. He was simply helping to guide his blatantly inebriated companion home to sleep it off. The boy obviously wasn't used to liquor. He certainly wasn't used to an older man plying him with it.

Back at the little flat Fritz called home, there was a lot of clutter, a lot of cases not so different from the one that the boy had dropped off there in passing. So many things belonging to so many boys, and he was too drunk to see them, or to understand what they meant.

Maybe there was still some reluctance in the boy when he felt Fritz's lips pressing on his own. Maybe he tried to pull away, to stop the deft fingers working down the buttons of his shirt. This was something that would forever be a secret. It didn't matter how progressive or cosmopolitan things in Germany were getting, this was never going to be some bold romance to brag about to his friends back home. This was a meeting of circumstance and necessity. New in town, lost and alone, the boy needed somebody to take care of him.

Fritz dropped down to his knees in front of the teen, fumbling at his belt buckle. His excitement starting to get the better of him. The boy was slim, but in between the drapes of his open shirt, Fritz could see some hints of muscle. There was enough meat on him to serve all of Fritz's purposes. He mouthed his way down the boy's stomach and the downy hair just starting to grow there. Listening to the moans and groans.

Whatever reluctance there had been before, it was all gone now. Heat had washed through the boy, chasing any doubts away. Not every moment of his life needed a song sung about it. Not every encounter had to be the next great romance of his life. Things worked differently for men than when there was a girl involved. It was more straightforward, less complicated, sometimes it meant something, sure, but sometimes it was exactly what it looked like and nothing more. As Fritz yanked his trousers and underwear away, the boy realised that somewhere in the fumble they had made their way to a bedroom.

The bed was old, the mattress sagging, but so long as it held their weight, the boy didn't give a damn anymore. He was lost in the spin of the kisses and the gin.

If he'd been just a little more aware, he might have wondered about the smell in the room. Not the smell of sex, which would have been entirely expected, even when they first arrived. Fritz hadn't made any pretences about what he was and what he wanted in that regard. Instead, there was a smell that would have, at first, seemed unfamiliar. A metallic tang in the air that wasn't quite strong enough to be easily recalled, but which eventually could have been put together with the smell of a butcher's shop. It wasn't the rot of old death or the harsh horror of new. It was a place saturated over days, months , or years, with spilt blood. Butchered meat.

The kind of guy who would buy you a drink and pick you up in a bar was not the kind of guy who would do the things with their mouth that Fritz was now doing. How should a kid, young and nervous, know how to reciprocate? His previous experiences may well have been brief, brutal, back-alley dealings, and that was if he was lucky enough to have found anyone at all. The distinction between sexual roles was traditionally fairly rigid. Maybe he would pass it off as an oddity, maybe he'd assume that the people in big cities were just more flexible about what they'd be willing to do together. Either way, it wouldn't be the truth.

Fritz just wanted the sensation of flesh in his mouth. As he worked his way back up the boy's body, his kisses had turned to open-mouthed bites, hot and raking over the flesh, but not finding purchase. Up he went, creeping closer and closer to the boy's pretty face. Away from those parts of him that some part of Fritz's mind was already filing away as meat. He turned the kid by his chin to seize one more kiss.

When he reared back from him, the boy was lazy-eyed and punch-drunk with lust. Fritz could not remember ever having seen anything quite so beautiful. He could feel his jaws spreading wide, his neck coiling back like a serpent ready to strike, all as though he were just a passenger in his body, watching what was unfolding, instead of the person in control. This was what he wanted. This is what he came for. Not the kisses, or the fumbling touch of a teenage boy, but this moment.

He lunged down, and his teeth met.

Mother's Boy

Fritz was born in 1879 to Johanna and Olle Haarmann. He was their sixth and youngest child and would prove to be their last, as his mother's continually declining health made it impossible for them to have any more after him. Indeed, giving birth to Fritz was very nearly the last thing that she would do, and it would be several weeks before she was finally released from hospital, returning home with her newborn in tow.

Olle Haarmann had carried a relatively dark reputation into the marriage, with many townsfolk whispering that his marriage to a woman in her forties had far less to do with late discovered love, and considerably more to do with the inheritance she had received, and the substantial dowry that would accompany her arrival into his life. She was seven years his senior when they were wed, and the fact that she managed to produce six children at her age was nothing short of miraculous in a time before science had done much to assist in matters of fertility.

Having numerous children at her relatively advanced age left Johanna as something of an invalid, constantly haunted by assorted health problems. She was often bedridden, and even when she was not, she certainly did not have the energy to be roughhousing with her boys.

By comparison, Olle was rarely around for long enough to even acknowledge his children's existence. The way he told it, he worked every single hour that God sent just to be able to pay for them. The sad truth, however, is that he spent much of his time and energy indulging himself with an elaborate series of extramarital affairs punctuated by long alcoholic benders that left him sleeping it off on public benches when none of the ladies he courted would allow him in their beds.

On those infrequent occasions when he was home, he generally ignored his children entirely unless they managed to catch his eye with some irritating behaviour. When this happened, his temper would flare. He was a harsh disciplinarian and would not hesitate to flog the children within an inch of their lives. He seemed to hate every single one of them, but given his reputation in town as 'Sulky Olle', it seemed that he had the same attitude toward literally every human being who ever had the poor fortune to encounter him. Johanna, he neglected or verbally abused, seemingly without pattern. When she became aware of his affairs, after he brought syphilis into the marital bed, he doubled down on his abuse rather than expressing repentance or showing any sign of guilt. It was her fault that he had strayed, with her lazing around all day, her body drained and unhealthy, in a state of slow decay. It was no surprise at all that he'd seek physical affection elsewhere when she barely had the stamina to stand up on most days. He was repulsed by her, and she was so worn down by years of verbal and psychological abuse that she accepted it as her due. She forgave or forgot about his affairs almost as soon as she learned about them.

Into all of this came young Fritz. The apple of his mother's eye. The bane of his father's existence.

Unlike his older brothers who were quite happy to follow their father's example and ignore their mother entirely, heading out the door of the house at the crack of dawn to go frolic and fight in the garden and streets all day long, Fritz spent most of his time in her company.

He was a quiet child, introverted and fine-featured. When the other boys invited him to play, he had tried but had found all of their rough games to be unpleasant. When his older sisters wanted to play with dolls, he would be there in an instant, joining in, and having a truly marvellous time. He even became their doll himself, getting dressed up in their hand-me-down clothes as they painted him with their mother's makeup. He was the perfect little plaything for them when they wanted to play house, a living doll who was happy and compliant with whatever they might ask of him.

The boys saw his interest in dolls and sisters as a personality flaw, distancing themselves from him. Their father's overbearing sense of what was and was not masculine defined them, and they learned to loathe their youngest sibling for his effeminacy. As he grew older, Fritz continued down this same path. Helping his mother in the kitchen and developing a passion for cooking and other 'women's work' like sewing. He helped his sisters to sew dresses for their dolls, and later for themselves. He practised needlepoint, creating beautiful little cross-stitch designs that his father would throw away in disgust upon learning who had made them.

His shyness around the boys soon extended to the girls of his family too, until his only social contact was his beloved mother. In him, she saw some sort of kindred spirit, a soft and gentle soul in a world full of those who were anything but. She cherished her littlest son, and in so doing spoiled him very badly. He only needed to ask for something and it would be given to him. Since the majority of the family money came from his mother, she held the purse strings. As such, little Fritz was always the one to have new shoes, new clothes, any toy that he might ask for, while his older siblings had to demand and whine to get what they wanted, often needing their father to intercede on their behalf. This was a dangerous game. It was just as likely to end with them receiving a beating for their temerity to speak to him as it was for them to see their father take out his frustrations on their mother, instead.

Resentment grew among the children until Fritz was essentially excommunicated from the family by his siblings. Loved only by his mother. Cared for only by his mother.

In response to this rejection, Fritz began to frighten the other children. If he could not have their love, then he would have their terror. By night he would creep from his bed, outside the house, and tap upon their windows. In the morning when they came down to breakfast looking tired and haunted, he would further their unease by sharing stories of ghosts and werewolves. When given the opportunity to 'play' with his sisters, he now more often than not contrived reasons to tie them up and then abandon them in such bondage for long periods, to the point that the girls sometimes soiled themselves before they could be rescued.

This image of him as a prankster was instilled in the children of the neighbourhood, and while he never properly socialised with the other children, many of them seemed to develop a begrudging respect for the torments that he inflicted on others. Many of them soon became victims of his desire to cause fear, and rarely would a day pass without little Fritz leaping out of some dark corner to draw screams from the unsuspecting children.

When he started school, the situation did not improve. His teachers reported him to be a mollycoddled and spoiled brat of a boy, accustomed to getting his way and liable to sulk if he did not get it. He was also prone to daydreaming, meaning that he lagged behind in his studies. He behaved well enough in class, but he could not interact with his peers in any sort of meaningful way. This was exacerbated by his odd behaviour, showing up to school on multiple occasions dressed in his sisters' old uniforms, and his constant desire to evoke fear in not only the children of his year but the younger ones too. He was not considered a bully, as such, because to be a bully he would need to have targeted specific individuals. His campaign of terror was non-specific and widespread.

His lack of social skills, his unusual behaviour, and his unsatisfactory academic progress eventually resulted in him being held back for a year, further isolating him from his peers and placing him in constant contact with children considerably younger than him. This provided an excellent opportunity for him to hone his talent in scary stories and practical jokes, yet another nail in the coffin of his learning to act his age.

When he was about eight years old, Fritz had his first homosexual encounter. Not with one of his peers as might have been expected, but rather with one of his teachers. This man, entrusted with the care of young children, molested Fritz when he chose to stay inside the classroom rather than go outside to play in inclement weather with the rest of his classmates.

It was the sort of traumatic event that would have completely changed the course of most young boys' lives, but for Fritz, it barely seemed to have left any impact at all. Nothing about his behaviour or attitude changed. Nothing in his school life or home life was altered in the slightest. Even years later, he would only mention the event in passing, as little more than an anecdote rather than a serious complaint. It seemed that even at that age, his perception of what was normal was warped beyond all recognition.

By the age of fifteen, he was done with school. He had seen no benefit from it throughout his life, considered it to be a waste of time, and his Luddite of a father did not differ in his opinion on the matter. Still, he insisted that Fritz must find something to do with his life. His brothers had gone from school straight into jobs, connected through a social network of their peers to business owners throughout the town, progressing through apprenticeships and well on their way towards impressive careers. Fritz came out of schooling with nothing on the horizon.

Through his father's business connections, Fritz was placed in an apprenticeship with a locksmith in the walled city of Neuf-

Brisach but was returned home in disgrace shortly afterwards. His employers would not speak of what rules he had broken, or what specifically he had done to earn their ire, but the general rumour-mill consensus back in Hanover was that he had displayed some sort of grotesque moral failing that had led to the man no longer wishing to teach him the breaking and making of locks.

Fritz was now confronted with the cold reality of being trapped at home under his father's constant observation. That's why the domineering man's next suggestion was actually something of a relief. If the boy could not make a decent showing of himself in civilian life, then perhaps a little bit of military discipline might improve him.

The idea of a military career for Fritz may have sounded laughable to those who knew him as a child, but now on the cusp of manhood, his appearance had quite thoroughly changed. He was a trim and physically strong young man who would not look even a little out of place in uniform. The idea of a structured career where everything was decided for him also appealed to him, given how rudderless he had felt throughout so much of his life. His mother's health was in another downward spiral, and he likely would have stayed by her side if it were not for the fact that she had given him her blessing to pursue this course.

On the 4th of April 1895, he began his military training at the academy in the town of Breisach. To everyone's surprise, and none more so than his own, Fritz adapted perfectly to military life. The strict discipline and schedules ensured that he had no time for his mind to wander. The drills and combat training came as naturally to him as swimming to a fish. For the first time in his life, Fritz was not only considered to be doing an acceptable job, but he was excelling. There were murmurs among the resident trainers that he was likely to depart their institution with a field commission and could become an officer with just a little bit of experience under his belt.

His future was just starting to open up in front of him when tragedy struck. During patrol, he was found staring off into space with the typical daydreaming expression that he'd borne so often during his schooling. His sergeant dressed him down for behaving in such a manner when he was supposed to be on duty, but it was only in the midst of that yelling that Fritz seemed to come back to himself, confused and dismayed. After several more similar episodes, he was remanded to the care of the medical corps where it became clear that his problem was not a mere lack of mental focus but some sort of neurological issue.

At first, the medical staff believed that he was suffering from some sort of anxiety neurosis, overwhelmed by his new military life and all the trials and tribulations that went along with it. But even when he was given bed rest and complete peace of mind, the symptoms persisted. It would only be months later that they would realise that he was, in fact, suffering from something akin to epilepsy and that these blanked-out periods where he seemed to lose all awareness of the world around him were not bouts of daydreaming, but seizures. In October he discharged himself from the military rather than waiting to be discharged on medical grounds. He did not want to live as an invalid off the pension that the army would provide. Instead, he returned to Hanover, explaining very little about the situation to his incensed father, but politely requesting that the man find him some work in one of the businesses that the family owned.

In 1888, Olle had taken a not-insubstantial portion of his wife's fortune and opened up a cigar factory in Hanover, a place where he worked most days that he was not out carousing and drinking. It was there that he decided to place his youngest son so that he could keep an eye on the boy and make sure that whatever problems Fritz had caused in both the locksmithing and army businesses would not affect his bottom line.

As it turned out, Fritz was as diligent a worker as his father could have hoped for. His co-workers ignored him for the most part, knowing as they did that he was the boss's son, but if they had expected him to receive any special treatment from the scowling older Haarmann then they clearly did not understand the man at all. There was no harsher critic of Fritz's work than his father. Had any other member of the shop floor been treated with the kind of disrespect that Fritz was bombarded with daily, then they'd have been liable to quit on the spot. But Fritz persisted. He took his father's abuse, his niggling over every minor error, and he worked his way up from the bottom of the factory. Starting as one of the boys that swept up loose tobacco from the floor and finally making his way up through the ranks to having machinery of his own to operate.

As his station in life grew, so too did his confidence, and his willingness to stand up to his father. When the man threatened to have the boy committed to a mental asylum during one argument, Fritz swiftly snapped back that he would sooner see his father in jail. It seemed that in his youth, Fritz had spent some of his endless alone time listening in on the conversations that his father had with colleagues. The man had started out in life, before benefitting from his wife's impressive dowry, by working on the trains - stoking the coal engines. During one heated argument aboard a train, he had gotten into a brawl with the driver. By the time the train arrived at the next station, that driver was nowhere to be seen. The elder Haarmann told police that he had left the driver on the train and disembarked to go drinking. In private conversations, however, Fritz had heard his father admit to killing the man and throwing him from the moving train.

Neither man was in possession of enough actual physical evidence to damn the other. They only had their words and recollections but even that seemed to be enough to ensure that neither father nor son would go too far with the other. Not with their reputations and freedom on the line.

Despite all that they had heard about him, through his hard work and determination, Fritz began to make a good impression on the people around him. All the rumours that had swirled around him, helped along by his father's constant and blatant disregard for the boy, started to recede. It seemed like he might have a decent life ahead of him. All it would take was a little more time, and he could have gotten out from under his father's shadow and started out properly on his own. Got himself a home, a wife, kids, everything an average man might have desired.

But then his true nature shone through.

Down into the Dark

At the age of sixteen, in July of 1896, Fritz was arrested for the first time.

While he had been building up his reputation among the people of town as a decent human being, earning their trust and their respect, he had also been doing utterly unspeakable things in those hours that he was not toiling away in the cigar factory. Many of the children in the surrounding neighbourhoods knew him as more of a peer than as an adult, and they were quite flattered when he offered to play with them, to teach them adult games too. Secrets that little boys were not meant to know, but that he was willing to share with them, because he liked them so much, if they promised that they could keep it a secret

He would lure individual boys that had strayed too far from their friends to secluded places, typically the basements of the blocks of flats near where he stayed. There he would proceed to strip them out of their trousers and molest them in much the same manner that he had been molested as a young boy.

True to their word, none of the boys shared the grown-up secrets that Fritz had inflicted upon them, but the physical toll of his games soon became apparent to several of the boys' parents.

Over a length of time and after much discussion, the parents eventually identified Fritz as the culprit.

Once it was reported to the police, it rapidly became public and many more parents came forward with their accusations. With considerably more sense of self-preservation than he had shown to date, Fritz turned himself over to the police before a mob of enraged parents could tear him apart. It was at this point that Fritz was charged with multiple counts of molestation.

As fate would have it, Fritz came across as rather strange to the police. He seemed even more off-putting than the heinous nature of his crimes would suggest. Consequently, the police did not feel comfortable holding and charging him without first having him undergo some form of psychological evaluation. The Division of Criminal Matters had him moved from the jail where he was awaiting trial to a mental institution in the city of Hildesheim in February of 1897. Though he was briefly sent back to Hanover hospital for further psychiatric evaluation, it was ultimately determined by Doctor Gurt Schmalfuß that Fritz was incurably deranged and would be unfit to stand trial in a court of law as he did not understand the consequences of his actions. Instead, he was to remain within the mental institution of Hildesheim until the end of his life should he not recover to a degree that would allow for his safe integration with the rest of society.

His parents signed him over permanently to Schmalfuß's institute in May of 1897, assuming that they would never see, nor hear from him again. For his father, this was the best possible outcome that he could have hoped for. For the continually ailing Johanna, it was an absolute nightmare. Her favourite son was being condemned as the worst sort of criminal. Even worse, he was being characterized by the world as so criminally insane, despite her having raised him so lovingly and to the very best of her ability, that he could never be allowed to be seen in public again.

To her delight and surprise, she began to receive letters from her son less than a month after his incarceration. It seemed that security was sufficiently lax in the institute that he could have mail sent out without any serious intervention or censorship on the part of his keepers. He explained that everything that had happened was a terrible misunderstanding, that he was being bullied out of town by a conspiracy led by his father.

Johanna believed every word.

She had always known that her husband hated her baby. Always known that he looked down on him as inferior to their other children and treated him even worse than he'd treated her through the years. She could feel her end rapidly approaching now, the strength that had once animated her was fading fast. The sharp pangs of her various ailments were growing ever more potent. Yet in her despair, she found fresh defiance. All her married life she had spent kowtowing to a man who would have been nothing without her fortune. A man who had treated her like an afterthought and treated the children, whom he should have loved, like a burden. And now he meant to be rid of the one child that his poisonous words had not taken hold of? She was not going to let it happen. Not while she still had breath.

After seven months of captivity, Fritz made his escape from the institution. It was patently obvious that he had been dismissed from his role as an apprentice locksmith due to being caught engaged in the molestation of children rather than due to any failure in his skills because there was not a single door in the whole of the institution that could withstand him once he had retrieved a set of tools from a janitor's closet. Quiet as a mouse, he crept from corridor to corridor, room to room, locked door to locked door. Unseen, unheard and unnoticed as he burrowed his way out through the heart of what should have been a fortress keeping the criminally insane away from the rest of the world.

All of this, he could have done at any time, but the next phase of the escape plan had eluded him. He did not have money, nor did he have any friends that he could rely upon to see him off to safety. Once he was outside of the institute in Hildesheim, he should have been stranded. Instead, when he clambered over the building's imposing gates he found a horse-drawn carriage waiting for him. Inside the carriage was a carefully packed suitcase containing all his clothes and worldly belongings along with a not-insubstantial sum of cash.

Under the cover of darkness, he was driven with all haste out of the town, and then on and on over the following days until he crossed the border into Switzerland. It was not until he arrived at the largest city, Zurich, that his final destination was revealed to him. A cousin and close friend of his mother, having heard from her letters about the terrible situation that he had found himself in, had offered up her home as sanctuary to the poor persecuted lad. He was in a new country, one that would not extradite him back to Hanover, even if a formal request was made, and he was granted a fresh start to boot.

The new living situation in which Fritz found himself fostered the feeling of being helplessly subject to the whims of instability. This sensation undermined his confidence enough to dissuade him from pursuing his darker interests. He did his best to avoid notice as much as possible. He sought out gainful employment and, to his surprise, soon found full-time work as a handyman at the local shipyard.

It was there that he encountered other people like him for the very first time. At first, it was the odd whistle here and there. An off-colour joke that portrayed one of the other men as something less than masculine, but not as something contemptible. Even as he tried to feel out his co-workers and get to grips with what they were implying themselves to be, they were doing the very same to the muscular, handsome, and yet subtly effeminate, Fritz himself. This slow dance went on for weeks, with the men inviting him to come out drinking with them, to visit specific bars and hotspots that would have been immediate giveaways to locals but which meant absolutely nothing to the German. He declined all invitations, still intent on living as quiet a life in Switzerland as he could manage, but their invitations went on getting more and more jovially insistent. It was as though they were all in on some joke that he wasn't privy to.

When he finally threw caution to the wind and agreed to go out for one drink at what turned out to be Zurich's premier gay bar, it was an eye-opening experience for him. He was so stunned by the things that he was seeing that he did not even manage to act as though he were repulsed or disinterested, as his father would surely have done. The shock of seeing men and women openly together was enough to silence the commanding voice that had echoed in his mind since he was barely old enough to speak.

All at once, his shipyard friends' jokes suddenly made perfect sense to him. He now understood what it was they had been trying to offer him all of this time. A friendly welcome was easy to come by in Zurich's tightly-knit underground community. A community that was more than willing to open its arms, and considerably more, for the handsome young German man.

He dipped in and out of the gay scene of Zurich many times in the months that followed, drawing in closer before being repulsed away by something that he had always been told was wrong. Everything that he knew about the world was challenged by the people that he met there quietly living their joyful lives. All of the happiness and pleasure that he had thought he could only find through harming others was right there, waiting to be taken, if he could only find the courage to let go of the man that his father wanted him to be, and become the man that he truly was.

The temptation proved to be too much for him. Time and again he found himself drawn back into the underworld of men in makeup and women in suits, trading kisses with strangers, running his hands across bodies that he was not meant to desire. That nobody was meant to desire. That it was twisted and wrong and sick to desire, just like his father had made sure that he knew. The lessons taught by the belt stuck around longer than the scars that the buckle had made.

It was too much. So long as he knew the opportunity was there, he knew he was going to get drawn back into the waiting arms of lovers and friends. The first ones he'd ever known in his life, who saw his strangeness as a thing of beauty instead of a reason to persecute him. None of them was without sin, so none cast the first stone. Even if he had gone to them and admitted to all of the awful things that he had already done in his life, there was no question that he would find forgiveness and acceptance. Forgiveness that he had not earned. Acceptance that he did not deserve. He was a monster. Every bit the twisted pervert that his father had always said he'd turn out to be.

He was sick, and this place was only making him sicker. He had to leave. Even if it meant facing the consequences of his actions back home, he couldn't stay so close to temptation. He had to make a clean break with Zurich and the people that he had found there. He had to go home and make a new life for himself as the kind of man that he was meant to be. The kind of man that could make his father proud of him.

He had remained in Zurich for over a year, but at the sixteen-month mark he offered his thanks and his apologies to his once-removed cousin and set out for Hanover. He had with him the remainder of the nest egg his dear mother had provided along with the meagre amount of his handyman wages that had escaped being drunk in seedy bars. He was willing to face the music if he must, but more importantly, to escape the far more insidious danger that he had found here in this place. The danger that wore joy as a mask and used love like a dagger straight to his heart.

In April of 1899, he arrived back on his parent's doorstep. His mother ushered him in without a word, as though his presence might have been overlooked if it were not spoken of, but his father caught sight of him anyway and erupted into blind rage at the presence of his evil spawn.

As a man was meant to, Fritz endured the beating, holding out until there was a break in the seemingly ceaseless diatribe that his father was unleashing upon him to announce that he had been released, that he was cured, that the things that he had done before were caused by an affliction of the mind from which he no longer suffered. He would have told them any lie at that moment to make the violence stop, but he just so happened to hit upon the one that resonated with both his mother and his father.

She wrapped him up in her arms, now so thin that he swore he could see the bones moving beneath paper-thin skin, and even his father, who loathed him like nobody else on earth could see that the boy was serious in his statement. He truly meant to start over. Even knowing that his reputation would never recover from the tales of what he had done, he was willing to face the world head-on. If Olle Haarmann had been capable of feeling pride in the actions of any of his children, then that might very well have been the moment that he would have done it.

The one beating was all hc received from his father, and that wasn't much of one compared to all the thrashings he had previously endured. Surprisingly, he found himself treated with something almost resembling filial attention. His father placed him in a back-office job in one of his other businesses, out of sight and out of mind, so that nobody had the opportunity to seek him out or seek vengeance against him. Tempers had cooled in the intervening years but many of the parents that would have sought Fritz's death before would soon be reaching for pitchforks and torches again if it were discovered that he had sidled his way back into Hanover.

For a time, all was quiet in the lives of the Haarmanns. Fritz went through the motions and did all that he could to make his father proud. He crushed all of his desires and dreams down until they were compacted so deeply that they were as dense and heavy as solid lead. Still, he knew that the old man was probably looking upon him with suspicion and doubt. He needed to do more. He wanted to prove that he was the kind of manly man that his father had always wanted him to be. It didn't matter how personally distasteful he might have found it. He needed his father's approval above all else.

Early in 1900, he found the perfect opportunity to prove the kind of man that he was.

Erna Loewert was a local girl a few years his senior, who was reportedly quite pretty, but unfortunately built to a slightly larger scale than other women of the time. As such, while her peers were all settling down to get married, she remained on the shelf, so to speak. At least until Fritz came along and dazzled her with constant displays of the kind of romance she had only read about. Most of the other girls who were her peers would not have been taken in so easily by Fritz, but the truth of the matter was, she was hungry for the kind of love that he was offering her, and she had no good reason to turn him down. Not when he looked at her like she was the answer to every problem that he'd ever had. Not when he was so kind and respectful and barely laid a hand upon her without prompting.

The two families met and were united in relief that the young lovers had found one another. The Haarmanns hoping that their wild and wicked son would find his worst impulses tempered by the kind touch of a woman, and the Loewerts simply delighted that their daughter was not doomed to become an old maid and miss out on all the joys that life offered a woman.

The two were engaged to be married soon afterwards, and everyone thought that it was absolutely wonderful that the two of them were taking that step. At least until Erna's pregnancy began to show. While Fritz had been unwilling to do anything that could have been considered untoward without a specific invitation, it seemed that his bride-to-be had been more than inviting. Repeatedly.

Yet even as her stomach swelled and Fritz faced his future as a husband and father with mounting trepidation, the world around them did not come to a halt. Now that he was returned to Hanover, Fritz was living the life of a German citizen once more, which meant that like all young men in Germany at the time, he was expected to perform his compulsory military service.

Seizing on this opportunity, Fritz immediately departed from Hanover to begin his conscription in the Alsace region, abandoning Erna only a few months before they were to be wed and before their child was born. He may have dressed up his decision in the garb of patriotism, but it was apparent to everyone involved that this was an act of sheer cowardice. His father almost intervened on poor Erna's behalf, drafting a letter explaining the situation that should have seen Fritz relieved from service, but Fritz refused to be party to such 'fraud.'

The first time that he had been in the army had been the last time that he had felt truly content in his life, and if he now had an opportunity for a second chance at that, then there was no possibility, however remote, that he was going to throw it away for some girl he'd barely met, or some baby he'd never even seen.

Obviously, this was not the specific language with which he expressed himself or his father would have beaten him within an inch of his life. Regardless, for the good of the fatherland, Fritz departed in October to begin his service in the Alsatian city of Colmar with the Number 10 Rifle Battalion.

The Good Life

In his later years, Fritz would describe his time in Alsace as the happiest in his life. Surrounded day and night by athletic young men, he soon fell back into the groove of military service, picking up exactly where he left off. The discipline of military life eliminated so much of the everyday stress that Fritz experienced back home. Here he did not need to think for himself, did not need to make decisions that could change his life and the lives of others. There was service, and there were orders, and he relished them.

Before long, he was receiving notice from his commanding officers for his excellence. In particular, it seemed that he was an excellent marksman, scoring the highest among his company in their target practice. Out in the field during their company exercises, Fritz was the man that his fellow soldiers looked to when they wanted to see how things should be done. He was obedient in the extreme and filled to the brim with 'esprit de corps.' Showing a love and admiration for his fellows that was enough to bring a tear to the eye of even the most vicious drill sergeant.

Internally, Fritz was at peace for the first time in a long time. He was being the kind of man that his father had always wanted him to be, masculine and strong while avoiding all the pitfalls of civilian life that he really could not stomach.

Though he wrote often to his mother, and occasionally to the woman who was soon to be the mother of his child, talking about how he looked forward to seeing them again, in truth he fully intended to carry on from his compulsory military service and try to make a career out of it. This was where he belonged, not out there in all the chaos and confusion, but here, where his target was clear in front of him and all he had to worry about was doing exactly as he was told, when he was told.

The seizures that had plagued him throughout his youth seemed to have cleared up once he was out of his adolescence, and that meant that there was no good medical reason that he couldn't go on to be a career soldier. It was as though all the barriers and burdens in his life had fallen away.

When he was pulled out of the barracks by his commanding officer in the middle of the night, he thought that the jig was up. That one of the other soldiers had reported him for his lingering looks in the showers, that his near-miss with a medical discharge had been passed along to his commanders, that the story of how he had molested children back in Hanover had made its way here, that the accursed institution in Hildesheim had tracked him down and demanded that he be remanded back into their custody, even that somebody that he'd known from his sordid nights in Zurich had miraculously leapt over the border to damn him with an accusation. As it turned out, it was nothing so heinous. The officers only wanted to tell him the news in private so that he could get his emotions back under control before he faced the other men.

His mother had died.

The news of his mother's passing knocked the wind out of his sails. He didn't know what to say, what to do. Numbly he returned to his bunk in the barracks and slipped under the rough blanket. His eyes would not seem to close. He stared up into the springs overhead and tried to make sense of what he had just been told. His first impulse, as it always was when he was unsure of the next course of action he should take, was to write to his mother for her advice. But of course, he couldn't. She was gone.

The weight of it began to settle on his chest, pressing him down into the paper-thin mattress. She was dead. The one person in all the world that loved him. The only one who had ever cared. She was gone. He had left her behind to chase his dreams of being a soldier, and now he would never see her again. If he went back to the officers and begged, they might let him go to the funeral. To see his brothers and sisters and their husbands and wives, all mourning, or at least putting on a show of mourning. None of them had loved her as he loved her. And worst of all, presiding over the whole thing, would be his father. Olle Haarmann, the ringmaster of his own wife's demise. He may not have been the one to kill her, but he had been the one to drive her to despair. He was the one to infect her with his filthy cock. He was the one who had forced a woman past her prime to turn out child after child after child, even though her body could not take the strain. If there was any villain in this story, surely it was him.

Fritz couldn't do it. He couldn't face him. Not even for his dead mother. She wouldn't even be there to see him. She was gone. All that he'd be going back to were screaming and recriminations on all sides. He wasn't going to do it. He didn't care what people would think, or what people would say. They all already hated him. Their opinion of him had been poisoned by Olle before he was old enough to walk. Why should he waste his time courting their good opinion when it mattered nothing to him at all? Why should he care about any of them now that his mother was gone?

She was the only link in the chain that connected to him. With her death, that link was no more, he was cut loose. Finally, he was free of the family, free of his father, free of Hanover and all who dwelled there. The bride-to-be that he didn't want to touch. The child that he didn't want to father. The home that he didn't want to build. There was nothing there for him but sorrow and pain. So why would he ever look back? The future of Fritz Haarmann was here. He had made a new start for himself. He would continue down this road, become the man he was meant to be, a proud stalwart soldier in the German Rifles. A crack-shot marksman. Someone that the freshly conscripted young men could look up to and emulate.

With his jaw set, he forced his eyes shut. Regulations would have them up bright and early the next day for field exercises, and bad news or bad weather was no excuse for an inferior performance from the top boy of the unit.

He collapsed about midday.

The other soldiers in his unit scrambled to drag him into cover, even though they were certain the exercise would be called to a halt the moment the officers realised that somebody was actually hurt. When they tried to stir him, Fritz's eyes were rolled up into his head, and he began to shake. The epilepsy that had plagued his youth had returned in force.

The medics quickly arrived and Fritz was transported away with all haste to the nearest military hospital, where he soon regained consciousness and began spinning tales. Heat-stroke. Exhaustion. Any excuse for his ill-health other than the truth, that the seizures of his youth had come back to strike him down again in his time of stress and grieving. Believing the best of the young soldier, he was soon signed off and sent back to duty, but it would scarcely be a week before his constant 'dizzy spells' resulted in him hitting the ground once more. Over and over, he lost consciousness. And the more times that it happened, the more stressed he became. He knew that if the army discovered he had epilepsy, he would be gone before the end of the day. His career over. His hopes and dreams of a new life for himself dead in the water. It was the stress of that realisation that was exacerbating his seizures.

It wasn't long before he woke up from what he had thought was a normal day of exercises in the field to find himself in a hospital once more, with no knowledge of how he had come to be there. None of his officers was there waiting to drive him back to campus. None of the doctors or nurses would tell him anything useful. He was a prisoner there as they poked and prodded at him, trying to determine the exact nature of the ailment that continually robbed him of his awareness and cast him down.

The first time that he had gone through such tedious medical checks they had been cut off abruptly by his decision to abandon the army. Now that he had tasted the reality of civilian life, he clung to his confinement in the hospital as a welcome holiday. There was nothing left for him out there. Nothing he wanted. Nobody who cared about him.

He remained in the hospital for so long that eventually he was given a diagnosis of dementia praecox. This now-disused medical term typically translated as precocious madness or premature dementia has now been replaced with the general term schizophrenia. It was believed at the time to be an incurable and degenerative disease that would continue to disrupt Haarmann's cognitive functions, rendering him unable to focus, retain memories or pursue his goals. Pharmacology would not provide any sort of relief from these symptoms for decades to come, so at this point, with no more use to the army, he was discharged honourably with a relatively insubstantial disability pension of 21 marks a month with which to support himself.

On return to Hanover, he had fully expected to receive something of a cold shoulder from his wife-to-be, given how readily he had abandoned her and his newborn child, but he certainly could not have predicted how he was received. His father and the family doctor collected him from the train station and he was sequestered in a sanatorium cell before he had the opportunity to even understand what was happening. It was only after the doctor had him locked in the room that he finally explained the situation. Haarmann senior had received word ahead of time that his invalid son was returning home and that preparations should be made for his care. He interpreted this as an opportunity to see his problem child locked away out of sight and out of mind once more, with no pestering mother fighting to get him released. If Olle had his way, Fritz would never see the light of day again. He would remain permanently confined in the very same sanatorium to which he had been remanded the last time around. To achieve this goal, Olle Haarmann had devoted much effort to collating a dossier on his son. He painstakingly detailed every bit of evidence pertaining to all his son's wrongdoing and abnormal behaviour stretching clear back to childhood. He recounted every shameful detail of Fritz's unusual interactions with other children, his desire to molest boys, his abandonment of his family and his overt avoidance of sexual 'normalcy'. Even his close relationship with his mother was cast as some moral deficiency that had been caused by a malformation in his brain from birth.

For Olle, he was finally delivering the death blow to the monster that had been plaguing him throughout the years. For Fritz, it was an outright declaration of war when before their manoeuvering against one another had been subtle and hidden.

Unfortunately for Olle, it seemed that the town doctor, Dr Andrae, who had cared for young Fritz since before he was able to walk, had considerably more interest in providing the young man with a fair assessment rather than simply rubber-stamping his father's prepared warrant for his confinement. Over the course of hours and then days, he conducted as thorough a mental evaluation of Fritz as had ever been conducted. Poring over the notes from his previous period of confinement, examining the medical history that the army had provided for him and engaging Fritz in conversation about his criminal history rather than jumping directly to accusations and blame. Andrae did not manage to winkle any new information out of Fritz, but with time the young man relaxed enough to engage in the conversation and offer what justifications for his actions that he could.

By the end of it all, the doctor would not sign off on Fritz being shipped off back to the asylum. He considered the young man to be a homosexual, and therefore 'morally inferior' but he did not believe that he was mentally ill, or so far beyond help that he could not live a normal life with ample support from his family.

And so it was that Olle Haarmann had backed himself into a corner. By involving the local doctor, he had tied the success of his scheme to his reputation with the local community. If he now went off and tried to get Fritz committed through other means, then the doctor might speak out against him, accusing him of being unsupportive of a young man with health problems, rather than an imbecile or monster, as Olle had always tried to paint Fritz. The only thing that Olle could do to be rid of the boy was bide his time and wait for a better opportunity. For now, to avoid being the subject of local gossip, he would need to keep his vulnerable kin from the breadline.

At the grand age of twenty-four years, Fritz Haarmann was finally released to resume a free life. Yet he was entirely aware that his situation was as precarious as the financial support that he could now demand from his father. Public opinion would hold sway over him. If he lost the good opinion of the people in the community, then it would open him up to another attack from his father. If he was anything less than the ideal citizen, he was at risk. So instead of seeking out some solace, he was forced to move into an apartment with his bride-to-be and child. He had to pretend that he was a normal man, with normal interests, living within his means as best he could on the meagre pension he received from the government.

With a little financial support from his father, of course.

Olle Haarmann resented every mark that he had to turn over to his loathed son. If he could have made a performance of his charity and used it to prove to others that Fritz was incapable of managing his finances, then it would have been a different story, but between his honourable discharge and the doctor's intervention, he had no such luck. Still, if he had to pay his son like he was an employee, then Olle was going to do his damnedest to extract every ounce of labour from him like one too. He sent the man back to work in the cigar factory where he had once thrived, amongst the people that they had tried to shield him from after he had sexually assaulted their sons.

He was the son of the boss, so they had to tolerate Fritz, but that did not mean that he was welcomed back gladly. It was hard to imagine anyone in the whole city who was so reviled on a daily basis.

The conflict with his father dominated Fritz's thoughts to the point that he became an oddly pliant partner to his fiancée; a woman who had already suffered through the awful shame of having a child out of wedlock at a time when such things were considered unspeakable. Now she was forced to endure this man who had happily abandoned her in her time of need, a man who was so loathed by the people in her neighbourhood that it was scarcely safe for him to walk the streets by night without fear of reprisals. She took him back because she was given no real choice if she wanted to keep a roof over her and her child's head, but she had made it clear to Fritz that if he didn't step up and start providing for them in a more meaningful way, their relationship, such as it was, would be over.

Despite the fact that he was diagnosed with dementia praecox which would supposedly interfere with his ability to think clearly or plan his future, Fritz still managed to prove himself quite capable of some clever scheming. Within a few months of working in the cigar factory, he had filed a suit against his father using the family lawyer, demanding disability pay and maintenance paid to him as a medically discharged veteran being forced to work in a job that he was physically incapable of undertaking.

This marked the first time that Fritz attempted to use the legal system to take revenge upon his father rather than simply degrading his parent's reputation through his actions. When the papers were served to Olle it almost resulted in a physical brawl. This was something, it seemed, that Fritz was not only anticipating, but relishing. He made sure to position himself somewhere public so that when his father arrived, screaming and raving at him, everyone in town was there to see it. When his father raised a fist to him, he simply lifted his chin and smiled in anticipation. If he could have his father arrested for assault it would only lend more credence to his suit. It would provide evidence that his employer was hostile towards him, and deliberately put him into situations that would do him harm. It was only the swift intervention of Olle's business associates dragging him off that prevented

Fritz from winning his suit instantly in the court of public opinion.

By the time the suit finally reached court, Olle had calmed down, hired himself competent representation, and was more than capable of proving to the judge that providing employment to his son, along with the other financial support that he had doled out through the years, was, in fact, a more than valiant attempt to support his 'morally inferior' son. Given what was known of Fritz by the court, courtesy of the vast dossier that his father had prepared, it did not take much for the ruling to come down against Fritz.

Thwarted in what he had thought was a perfect way to secure the extra funds that would get Erna off his back, and now suffering from the loss of income following his summary dismissal from the cigar factory, Fritz was backed into a corner.

He switched tactics to manage the situation, becoming the perfect husband to Erna in every sense except for the legal one. Unfortunately, this pretence put additional strain on his already frayed mental health.

Well aware that anything resembling illegal behaviour could very well result in his return to the asylum, Fritz could not fall into old habits. Whether he committed robbery to resolve his financial issues, or molestation to ease the internal tensions, he would have been putting himself back into his father’s crosshairs and handing the man all the ammo that was needed to put him down.

Left with little other option to make ends meet, he finally went crawling back to his father to ask for another job.

The conversation did not go well. They met in the family home which was now as silent as a tomb after the death of Fritz's mother. All Fritz's siblings had long ago departed to start their own lives. Olle endured Fritz's presence only long enough to be certain that he hadn't missed any opportunity to make the boy suffer further indignity before he told him "no". He would not be providing Fritz with another job, not after the way that the boy had bitten the hand that fed him last time.

Fritz had come prepared with arguments highlighting how his dire financial situation had driven him to pursue the lawsuit and about the needs of his young family. Olle did not give a damn. He had not the faintest hint of concern for his son's problems. The boy had betrayed him, and there would not be another handout in the offing any time soon. He considered the whole thing to be tantamount to sheer laziness. Fritz wanted to live without having to work – the greatest of sins in Olle's eyes – and as such he should be forced to go out and seek employment on his own instead of coming to his father with his hat in his hands.

Needless to say, this did not sit well with Fritz. He had not come begging for money but, instead, had come asking politely for assistance in finding a job from a man who had more businesses in his portfolio than most of his employees had hot dinners. He felt that he had already proven himself to be quite capable of working for his pay when given the opportunity, even excelling in whatever role his father had slotted him into in the past. So, it was difficult for him to take this refusal as anything less than a personal attack. Which, in fairness, it was.

The argument escalated, with neither of the stubborn men willing to back down from the other, and both now feeling that the other was trying to deliberately do them harm out of unmitigated spite. This continued until, finally, the elder Haarmann had enough and fell back into his old ways raising his fist against his youngest child, as he had so often before. The difference was that Fritz was no longer a cowering child. He was now a full-grown man, a trained soldier and he'd suffered a lifetime of abuse from his father to fuel his rage. When Olle swung for him, Fritz hit him square in the jaw and knocked the older Haarmann on his ass.

The shouting had been enough to concern the neighbours and now that furniture was crashing about, the police were swiftly called in. By the time they arrived, the brawl had been resolved so firmly in Fritz's favour that it looked as though Olle had not been the instigator of the violence at all. The younger man was placed under arrest, but his father had no intention of pressing charges. Not when this played into his long-term plan so much more effectively.

This attack was evidence that Fritz was a danger to himself and others. It was grounds to have him sent off to the asylum once more. Olle filed his case for the young man's confinement citing attempted blackmail and verbal death threats which he allegedly received from his son. When the time came to provide evidence of these allegations, however, nothing could be found to corroborate his assertions. If Fritz had attempted to blackmail his father or threatened him with violence, it had been done in such a way that nobody ever heard it, no written records were ever made and it could not be proven. For his part, of course, Olle refused to even discuss what information his son might have had that could be used as blackmail material. His standing in the community would have been irreparably harmed if even the accusations of what he had done were to come out.

This in turn brought him to a moment of realisation. Much as he may have loathed his son and called his bluff time and again, the boy had never taken things so far as to do him actual material harm. Fritz knew enough about his business dealings, and in particular, the wet work that he had done when involved in the rail industry, that it would have been a simple thing for him to make his accusations public and ruin Olle's fortunes. Despite having suggested through the years, generally in the heat of an argument, that he might do just that, it had never come to pass.

Either the boy still maintained some affection for his father, or he saw him as too valuable a resource to permanently eliminate. Regardless, they were at an impasse, one where the tensions could only be eliminated by a move towards reconciliation on the part of Olle. He would have to be the bigger man, for the first time in his life.

Neither man apologised to the other, but gradually they returned to a state of equilibrium, and from there, Olle extended something of an olive branch towards his son. There were business opportunities out there for a young man, if Fritz were to present one of them to his father as a viable option, then the elder Haarmann would be willing to consider investing.

It was a gift, exactly what Fritz needed, exactly when he needed it. A job, an income, a future to build towards, all without having to endure the stifling presence of his father's looming shadow cast over him perpetually. He and Erna were ecstatic when he returned with the news and soon set about doing all their due diligence to find a viable opportunity in Hanover. With their combined experience, they finally settled upon a fishmonger as their business of choice and located both an ideal location for a shop, but also a supply chain to ensure that they would always be well stocked with fresh catches.

Taking their business plan to Olle, Fritz was half expecting to have the rug dragged out from under him. There was one small twist that he hadn't been expecting in the proceedings, but it was less of an attack upon him, and more a variable that he had not considered. Rather than registering the business in Fritz's name, buying the property in his name, or anything similar, Olle suggested that it all be put into the care of Erna. That way, Fritz could continue to claim his military pension without any accusations about his ability to work.

His father had always been sharp in terms of business, and Fritz was quick to agree to this amendment. As for Olle, he seemed delighted. The way that Fritz had treated his fiancée had always been one of the true crimes that Olle held against him, and he had now ensured that even if it became necessary to have his son locked up again in the future, she and his grandchild would still be taken care of.

Or as it would soon become, grandchildren.

In his efforts to placate his wife, it seemed that Fritz had been going above and beyond the call of duty, and she had fallen pregnant for a second time.

The fishmongers opened, and they did moderately good business from the outset. Given his unpopularity, Fritz stayed behind the scenes preparing and gutting fish all day long, while Erna, beloved by all in Hanover despite her poor choice of husband, was the face of the business. Fritz was overwhelmed with the immensity of their success until he realised that all the costs of running the business left them with only a fraction of their takings. At which point he began, instead, to panic. They had one child already costing a small fortune and a second on the way. They had all the fishhead soup that they could eat, but clothes, rent and all the rest added up rapidly. The initial booming business of the fishmonger began to ease as the novelty wore off, and soon the young couple was faced with the cold reality of being small business owners.

After much discussion, it was decided that there was not enough income from this single source to support the two of them and their two children. One of them would have to go and find an additional job to support the family. Given that Erna was the face of the business and that everything Fritz did occurred behind the scenes, and often at night, he was the ideal candidate.

The crowning touch to this latest indignity was that Olle began to help around the fishmongers on occasion. Not with the physical work of the job, such things were beneath a man of his stature, but with the paperwork and making deals with the suppliers. Erna couldn’t praise him enough for the help that he was giving them, but for Fritz, each little bit of help that he gave them was another twist of the knife.

The more that Erna came to appreciate his father, the more twisted Fritz’s perception of the situation became. He’d always been aware of his father’s womanising, of his pursuit of much younger women than were appropriate, even when he was married. Fritz started to draw lines connecting his father’s sudden change of heart in supporting Fritz's family and, especially, Olle's new annoyingly positive relationship with Erna. With the signing of all the business documents in her name. With the new pregnancy.

It was all entirely in his imagination. Olle’s interest in the fishmonger’s shop was merely a business one, a way to protect his investment and ensure a positive return on it. While it was true that he developed a good working relationship with Erna, often wondering aloud how such a sensible and well-put-together woman had ended up with his deranged runt of a son, there was nothing untoward happening.

Still, Fritz could not shake the feeling that he was being forced out of his home and business by Erna's demands that he go and seek work elsewhere. It was as though she were clearing out room for his replacement. Much like his father, her motivation was almost exclusively business-related too: Fritz was awful with the customers, and Erna had swiftly discovered that she could do his backroom jobs with considerably more efficiency and speed. He was surplus, redundant, unneeded. A drain on the family resources, contributing nothing. It felt like he was a child again, receiving all his father's loathing and contempt.

When he was hired on as an insurance salesman it seemed ideal. So long as he was successful, he would be bringing in a substantial amount of money in commissions to alleviate their financial struggles, and it would keep him out from underfoot so that Erna could get on with the running of the fishmongers without his attempts to be helpful causing her headaches.

The reality of the situation was quite different from that ideal, however. Fritz spent the vast majority of his time travelling away from home, and even when he was back in town, he rarely saw his wife, thanks to how busy the business was. His sales successes were surprisingly few and far between given that Germany was in the midst of an economic boom period. While his reputation no longer preceded him when he was travelling far afield, he now projected the persona of a man who was accustomed to being hated and ignored. Add to that the fact that he was often secretive and sometimes perceived as downright bizarre, he was not often well-received by prospective clients.

Making very little money and being far away from home much of the time, his suspicions about his wife's fidelity continued to mount. University students had begun frequenting the fish shop while he was away travelling, teased in by the kindly service and the low prices offered to them by Erna. In terms of business, the small discounts that Erna offered to students were soon overwhelmingly repaid by all the referrals from happy patrons. For his part, Fritz could not comprehend why people wanted to spend time with her, so he immediately jumped to the most sordid of conclusions.

Miserable, frustrated and exhausted from his work, he returned home to find a gathering of students lingering outside of the shop. It wasn't so much that the place had become a hangout for them, as that they just happened to bump into one another while doing their shopping.

It was the last straw for him. He barged past the queue, ignored the shouted greeting from his elder child and began bellowing a grotesque litany of betrayals at his fiancée. He accused her of cheating on him, of the children not being his, of forcing him to take on a job far from home so that she would have more time to conduct her affairs.

That, in turn, was the last straw for her. She had never been so humiliated and insulted in her entire life. The building, the shop, and their home were in her name. The children were considered hers alone under the law. When she broke off the engagement with him and told him to get out, she was well within her rights.

Fritz, so embroiled amid his outburst, didn't stop ranting and raving. He had a lifetime of vitriol to unleash and it was only when he finally realised that she had stopped talking and had gone back to serving customers as though he weren't there, that her words finally sank in.

His tune changed rather abruptly at this point. At first, trying to pass the whole thing off as some kind of test of her loyalty, then, failing that, descended into begging and pleading when the reality of the situation began to sink in. He had nothing of his own except for the case of clothes that went with him when he travelled for business. The building was hers, the business was hers, the apartment above it was hers, the children, hers. He had never taken on the responsibility of any of them, so he had never been granted any power over them. She was free to do as she pleased, and it pleased her greatly to eject Fritz from the premises with absolutely nothing to show for the life he had been trying so desperately to build with her except for the shirt on his back.

In desperation, he went running to his father, hoping that the old man could smooth things over and mediate some kind of reconciliation between him and his wife, or at the very least make sure he was given his fair share from the business he'd helped to found.

His father, predictably, laughed in his face and told him that he had been waiting since he first signed the finance papers for Erna to finally grow as tired of Fritz as he had been since the boy was but a toddler. This was the perfect outcome for Olle. He had a new business in his folio that was doing well, his grandchildren would be fed and housed, and his reputation would be secured no matter what Fritz said or did because now it was going to be clear to absolutely everyone that Fritz was the one who was the problem.

Fritz was the one who had thrown away a relationship with the mother of his children after refusing to do the right thing and marry her. Fritz was the one who couldn't run the business that his father had gift wrapped and handed to him. A business that some woman with no experience had turned into a profitable venture. All of the gifts that had been rained down on Fritz, he had thrown away and then had bitten at the hand that fed him. No more. Never again would Olle have to give a single penny to his least loved son. Never again would he have to endure the threats and blackmail. This was the killing blow to Fritz's credibility, and this was the last time that his father would ever have to speak to him again.

Double-Edged Sword

The final ties to his old life had been severed. Fritz emerged from his family home for the last time with no road map to guide him, but no force that could constrain him, either. All of his life, he had been limited by what his reputation would allow, how much misbehaviour his fiancée would tolerate, what his father would say, how it would break his mother's heart. But now all of those chains had been broken.

He might not have had a penny in his pockets, but what he did have was the perfect skill set to be a career criminal before he'd even taken the first step. Remaining in Hanover, he began to ply his trade, working alternately as a con man or burglar and slowly building up a network of connections in the criminal underworld that would have put his father's legitimate address book to shame. While he started out as the man to be called when there was a lock needing undone, he soon transitioned into a less active role, liaising with smugglers and illegitimate business interests outside of town for the fencing of stolen goods. He proved so valuable in this role that he scarcely had to undertake any actual breaking and entering after only a year or so. Bizarrely, the drive to succeed that his father had always felt was absent from his recalcitrant and most loathsome child now came to the forefront, and he used all of the things that his father had tried to instil in him through the years to develop his business in new directions.

To avoid undue scrutiny over his income, he attempted to take on some legitimate work through the years. As it turned out, his experience as both a business owner and in the wide variety of jobs his father had ungraciously provided in an attempt to keep him out of the way provided unexpected dividends in that Fritz found himself surprisingly qualified for any number of entry-level positions. While he would probably have chosen more physical jobs in his youth to assert his masculinity, he no longer felt compelled to pursue the ideal of heterosexuality that had been forced upon him for so long and was, instead, able to pick work that had the least physical impact, leaving him with more energy to pursue his other interests outside of work.

His first legitimate job was as a clerk in a government office, and to his delight, this in turn opened up new illicit opportunities for him in a variety of directions, both expected and utterly unanticipated.

In the realm of expected, he learned very quickly how to perform a variety of fraudulent activities within the office, allowing him to filter off funds to line his own pockets. In the realm of the unexpected, he met a female co-worker who recognised some sort of kindred spirit in him and soon began inviting him to spend time with her in the evenings.

At first, he believed that this was some sort of romantic overture, and he was quick to dismiss her and make his disinterest in such things clear. But gradually he came to realise that she simply wanted time to talk to him outside of the workplace and scope him out a little bit more thoroughly than office life would allow. She had become aware of his fraudulent activities in the office but was not attempting to blackmail him or get him into any trouble, in fact, she evened the playing field early by admitting to having made some fraudulent adjustments to the books through the years, herself. At first, he could not grasp why she would expose herself in that way, but slowly he came to understand that she was attempting to build his trust and get some understanding of just how flexible his morals might be. Since he had none, it didn't take long for her to get to the point.

She was a graverobber in her spare time. Digging up the dead, stripping them of valuables and selling them along. She didn't even require a fence most of the time since the victims of the robbery weren't making any complaints about her thefts. The trouble was, she lacked the physical strength and stamina to make much of the bountiful gardens arrayed around the churches of Hanover. She needed somebody to work with her to help with the heavy lifting, and she was more than willing to split the proceeds with whoever that lucky person was.

Fritz was feeling lucky, and with his connections as a fence, it was the perfect enterprise for him. He went out with his new friend to learn the ropes of robbing graves. Which ones were too old, with goods too spoiled. Which ones were too well tended, where any disturbance would likely be noticed.

When it came to the dead themselves, perhaps his new business associate might have assumed that there would be some squeamishness on his part, but Fritz took to it like a natural. He easily outshone his mentor with his complete lack of concern that a corpse lay between them. When fingers needed to be cut so a ring could be retrieved, he didn't hesitate. He had a butcher's skills from his time in the fishmonger's, and it was far easier to pop a half-decayed finger from its joint than to debone a fish. He tossed the bodies of the dead around as though they were nothing but an obstacle in his way, and if he ever even cared that they had once been living breathing people, it never showed.

Keeping up both that night job and his office work did not prove to be too taxing for Fritz, and both still left him ample opportunity to pursue his true passions in life.

It was actually because of that true passion that he was arrested and lost his clerical job early in 1905.

Without familial pressures or the masquerade of a happy engagement, Fritz had finally been able to pursue his love of young men. At first, he had limited himself to the same sort of encounters that he'd pursued when he was a young man. Isolating the young, tricking them into following him somewhere they wouldn't be heard and molesting or raping them. Reliant as always on the shame that those men felt at having been used in such a way to ensure that the crimes were never reported. As time passed, Fritz came to realise just how much freedom he now had and began to establish an entirely separate network of contacts in a not entirely separate underworld. Every one of the men that he got to know was, by legal definition, a criminal, but not in a way that his current crop of crooks and cronies would have recognised.

The underground gay scene in Hanover was not as accepted as the one that Fritz had encountered abroad, and his place in the ecosystem had drastically changed, as well. He was no longer the hot young thing that the older men were chasing, he was now the pursuer, competing with every other older man to convince whatever fresh meat was around that he would make it worth their time to give him their full attention.

It was not as easy to be an admirer as to be admired, and it was not so comfortable a role for Fritz to occupy. It felt predatory in a way that brought his non-consensual assaults to mind all too readily, and the fact that he had more success with the younger men that he was attracted to when he treated them like they were a mark to be preyed upon rather than a lover to be enjoyed just exaggerated that aspect of the pursuit. It was not long before he was looking upon potential lovers in the same way that he did the corpses that he robbed, working out the value of their valuables. It wasn't like they could report him to the police if he stole their watch while they were sleeping. Just being in bed with him was a crime, and nobody was going to willingly admit to it over some petty theft.

Eventually, however, he pushed his luck too far, burglarising a rooming house to where he had been invited by one of his young conquests. While the gentleman in question may not have been willing to press charges against him, there was no shortage of other residents who were happy to talk to the police about the criminal activity that had transpired between the two men if it meant they might get their belongings back.

A quick search of Fritz's apartment turned up a plethora of stolen goods from numerous burglaries around town, the majority of which, Fritz had not even been involved in. He was going to be serving time in prison regardless of what happened next, but at that moment, Fritz realised the potential power that he held over all his fellow criminals. By throwing one or two of them to the wolves, the police would reduce his sentence significantly.

It didn't even take him long to choose which of his so-called friends he was going to condemn. He had already assigned them varying values based on the other contacts that they could provide him, the quality of the merchandise that they brought to him, and how much he liked them. For a man who could dismember a corpse for a little extra walking around money, betraying his closest confidantes for convenience didn't even register on the scale of his morality.

While he did serve time for his crimes in this instance, it was a drastically abridged sentence compared to what he deserved, and while it may have cost him his job as a clerk, he was already making so much more from his criminal enterprises that holding his job down was already becoming a bothersome annoyance.

Fritz did not enjoy his time in prison, he never did, but he used the opportunity just as his father would have used a business conference, making connections that would pay off in the years to come. It was also his first experience of inter-prisoner romance. While he'd borne witness to acts of sexual violence before in his brief brushes with incarceration, he had not recognized the relationships of protection and convenience that older, stronger men would form with the young and beautiful. He had never seen long-term homosexual relationships before, even among those brief times when he dipped his toe into the underground dating scene. Here was a model that he could replicate in his own relationships, trading on his wealth and reputation as a criminal to attract someone that he wanted to keep. Admittedly, the vast majority of such relationships within the prison setting would be immediately forgotten about and denied the moment that their participants were set free, but for the fraction who were not willing to let go and forget, they could become lifelong, like a marriage.

Back in the real world, Fritz resumed his life of crime without hesitation. He settled by Hanover's Central Station and made it the new hub for his activities. The preponderance of smugglers that he dealt with travelled by rail making this an ideal place to observe all the new arrivals coming into town. This included the young men who might suit his tastes as well as criminals that might prove advantageous to recognise.

After his initial success at reducing his prison sentence through informing on others, Fritz had now developed a keen interest in those parts of the criminal underworld that did not directly impact his own business. There was not a police officer in all of Hanover with so encyclopaedic a knowledge of all the criminals who were in town, active, or wanted for certain crimes. Fritz was an affable and effeminate queer who fenced stolen goods and hooked other criminals up with jobs that might pay off down the line. He was trusted implicitly by a subsection of society that could only exist by being distrustful. What he didn't know, he could find out with laughable ease simply by engaging in a few conversations with the right people. Were he so inclined, he could have brought down every criminal enterprise in the city.

He was not so inclined.

Instead, he traded on information with the police, making a stop at the station a regular part of his daily rounds, where he would turn in tips and even arrange for the arrest of his competitors to a schedule aligned with his business interests. Of course, the police were not satisfied to ignore his crimes entirely in exchange for the steady flow of information, and that suited him well. He would schedule raids of his own apartment when he was having trouble shifting certain items, typically while one of his business associates was visiting. This gave the police the criminals that they needed, and also created a witness to Fritz's repeated arrests to attest that he suffered from the interest of the cops just as badly as all of the rest of them. He'd go in for a lenient sentence, and then pop back out again not long afterwards, right in time for anyone who had been angry with him for losing their stolen goods to have forgotten about it.

This cycle continued for years, Fritz became a fixed part of the Hanoverian ecosystem of crime, and when accusations made their way back to the police about him picking up young men, they turned a blind eye to it, because he was far more valuable out on the streets gathering intelligence for them than he was rotting in a cell just because young men didn't have the good sense not to accept help or drinks from a man like Haarmann.

However, there was a limit to the protection that could be offered to Fritz in exchange for his ongoing cooperation, and any public exercise of police power to protect him would have resulted in his immediate murder by the many people he'd betrayed. So, when he was caught in the act of robbing a warehouse in 1913, he was sentenced to a solid five years of imprisonment instead of the multi-month slaps on the wrist he had been receiving before then.

While he was furious and distraught at the time, it most likely saved Fritz Haarmann's life that he was in jail for those five years, because World War One broke out shortly after his confinement.

In the world outside of the prison walls, there was wholesale slaughter on a scale that had never even been conceived of before, let alone seen. Through a complex network of alliances and pacts, every nation in the world was drawn into the conflict, a war to end all wars, using modern technology to obliterate their fellow men in a manner more reminiscent of a slaughterhouse floor than anything so noble as battle. Poisonous gasses, barbed wire, disease, and explosives all played their part in bringing hell to earth, but ultimately it was men who kept the meatgrinder turning. Every able-bodied man in Germany was conscripted into service. As the war raged on and the losses mounted their definition of "able-bodied" began to expand. Teenagers and the elderly who were previously left in peace to keep the nation's cogs turning suddenly found themselves in uniform, out in the trenches on two fronts. Neither one of them hospitable.

Men died, and died, and died, the population of Germany decreasing so rapidly that it would take years before an accurate death toll could even be had. Fritz's brothers died. The boys he had molested as teenagers died. Everyone that anyone had ever known was more likely to be dead than alive, and still, the war raged on.

Had Fritz not been imprisoned, he would have doubtlessly been called to the front lines just as so many men of his generation were. Neither his military pension nor his disabilities would have spared him and when he inevitably proved to be incapable of performing, as had been the case with so many other men, he would have very likely died in the field or been summarily executed by a superior officer as an example to the other men. Such callousness was not unique to the German army, in fact, it was something of a standard practice at that time.

Prison absolutely saved his life, but the rewards of his criminality did not end there. Due to conscription, there was a massive lack of manpower to keep the country operating during the war. The trains still had to run on time, the food still needed to be harvested and the wealthy still wanted their homes to be maintained. It did not take the German government long to recognise the untapped potential contained in its prisons, and before long it began assigning jobs to those who were imprisoned for lesser crimes, like Fritz. While his countrymen bled and died across the globe, he became a gardener in the estates of the wealthy, released from prison each morning with no guard, on the condition that if he returned by nightfall he would be considered even more of a model prisoner, and allowed even more freedoms.

So, he would rise, eat a hearty breakfast and set off to do unsupervised work in the prettiest gardens of German aristocrats' estates, leaving when he pleased to get a drink with his friends, engage in whatever debauchery took his fancy, and then head back to prison for dinner and a good night's sleep. All while making a better wage than he had in any legitimate job he'd held down in his entire life.

Not only did Fritz find himself a very comfortable life thanks to his imprisonment, but he also got his first real taste of romance.

Hans Grans was in his early 20s when he was jailed as a pimp. He became friends with Fritz shortly after being incarcerated and found the older man's antics strangely endearing compared to the dour expressions of the other prisoners with whom he shared cells. The two were soon rooming together and spending almost every waking moment together too. Hans was not granted the same freedoms as Fritz, so it was very easy for the older man to spend some of the money that he was making to buy little treats for his sweetheart and smuggle them back into the prison. Essentially anything that Hans desired could be acquired for him, and while Fritz did not ask for anything in exchange, there was an implicit suggestion that should their relationship go beyond friendship, there would be even more rewards available to the young man.

Hans had lived a hard life, and he was not liable to look a gift horse in the mouth now that things were finally starting to go his way. While he may not have been homosexual in the same way that Fritz was, he was capable of enough flexibility to get what he wanted out of the relationship.

For Fritz, it felt as though the whole world had fundamentally changed. The things that other people had, he suddenly understood that he could have too. It would be different, because he was different, but he could still have love, a home, a family of sorts. He didn't have to spend his whole life alone, fighting against the whole world. Not when he had Hans by his side, giving him all of the love and affection that he had at first been denied, and then had denied to himself.

The freedom that had been afforded to Fritz during this latest jail sentence had not made him happy. No more than his crimes had made him happy, his children had made him happy or any other part of his life had ever made him happy. They felt less like a joy, and more often than not, like a burden. But here and now, he had found joy. In the body of the young hoodlum that he dared to say that he loved, he had found something that he wanted for himself, he had found a future for himself, something more than fumbles in dark alleys and outwitting the police so he could live to lie another day. It took his fear away.

For Hans, the relationship was different. It was more transactional. There can be no denying that he felt some measure of affection for the effete older man who had taken him under his wing and lavished him with luxuries that it was ridiculous to believe could be found within a prison's walls, but whether it was love or not, we will never know. It certainly wasn't the blind adoration that Fritz felt towards him. It didn't change the course of his life or make him wake up every day with a smile on his face. Manipulation had always been part and parcel of Hans' trade, and now for the first time, he found himself in a position where he could trade on his own flesh rather than that of the girls that he had ensnared through a web of deceit. He could choose to give himself to Fritz or to deny him, almost on a whim. He could choose to reflect all the love and affection that was being rained down on him, or to refuse it, driving Fritz into a frenzy of gift buying and praise. He may have been beholden to Fritz for everything that he had, but Hans controlled Fritz so thoroughly that nobody outside of the relationship would have believed who held the material power.

The only solace for Fritz throughout all of this was that his beloved was young, and his foot-stomping and attention-seeking ways were entirely in keeping with what he had seen of young brides, always demanding more and more of their husbands. To an outside observer, the relationship may have seemed ridiculous, doomed from the outset by the completely different angles that the participants were approaching from, but it seemed that Fritz was capable of infinite forgiveness when it came to his young love, and even when the pair of them were eventually set loose from prison, they did not part.

The world that they found was not the one that they had left behind.

The New World

In the time since they were incarcerated, the world war had changed everything, from the top of society all the way down to the filthy bottom feeders where they fit in.

Germany had lost. Despite all of their heroism, superior training, superior technology and superior tactical minds, they had been beaten by their opponents. But that was not enough for the powers of the Entente. The alliance of France, Britain and Russia wanted to see Germany punished for their audacity. As the youngest of the European nations, the old masters now sought to put Germany in her place permanently and ensure that she could never again amass enough power or resources to challenge them. While they had all of their vast empires and Germany had naught to draw on but the strength of its motherland, they had been badly bloodied in the fighting, to the point that fear more than rationality drove their decision-making when the time came to sign treaties of peace.

Germany was stripped of all the lands that she had taken in the fighting, even those that had now been settled by Germans for years. More importantly in the grand scheme of things, economic sanctions were enforced against her, and she was ordered to pay reparations for the damage that had been done in the fighting. For a country already on the verge of collapse after expending so much in the fighting, it went beyond crippling and into the realms of comical cruelty. There was no way that Germany could pay the tariffs being demanded of it in exchange for its ongoing existence. What they could not crush on the battlefield, the Entente now intended to slay through bankruptcy and starvation. There were no men to work the fields, no miners to dig the metals, even if there were still wealth buried in the land of Germany, they had not the means to reach it, and even if anything was found, it would likely have been plundered by foreign interests long before anyone in what came to be known as the Weimar Republic could feel any benefit from it.

It was into this desolate and starving Germany that Fritz and his lover emerged from prison. A world that seemed to be so changed that they could scarcely recognise it. At least at first.

There was a burgeoning black market in the Weimar Republic. All of the luxury goods that the wealthy of Germany had always enjoyed importing were no longer available through legitimate channels, which left those men who had previously dealt only in minor illegalities perfectly positioned to fetch them in. Fritz was already well acquainted with all of the smugglers of Hanover, but it was not there that he first travelled, but to Berlin, instead.

One of his older sisters lived there with her children, and Fritz had a mind to start fresh in a new city, now that his view on life had changed so drastically, he had wondered if he might not find legitimate employment to support himself and Hans, allowing his foul reputation back in Hanover to fade away.

They barely lasted a month before they went skulking back to Hanover with their tails between their legs. Without his contacts and his illegal businesses, it had been nigh on impossible for Fritz to make any sort of living. There was no shortage of legitimate businesses who were desperate to have him and more than willing to overlook his unsavoury past in exchange for the labour of a full-grown and healthy man. Unfortunately, while the amount that they were paying would once have been generous, the reality that they were now living in did not allow for such a simple exchange of work for wealth.

The price of bread would double in a day. People's savings were wiped out overnight. The value of the mark had dropped so low that the mint was forced to print larger and larger notes just to accommodate the rampant inflation. The only money of any value was foreign, and after a world war that had brought a crashing end to international trade by all legitimate businesses, the only ones who dealt in foreign money of any significant amount were the smugglers.

In an instant, those who had been on the periphery of society became the most sought-after. The ones who could get a bottle of champagne for a party, the ones who could give you a good price for your mother's jewellery when she passed. And at the centre of it all, there needed to be a ringmaster, an orchestrator, who could connect the smugglers and criminals with the people who sought them. A fence with a solid reputation, but a soothing enough manner not to scare the civilians away.

Fritz had another sister back in Hanover, to him they were essentially interchangeable anyway. Boring women with boring husbands and boring children that he couldn't believe they'd bothered to birth. He moved into her spare bedroom until he could get some money together to rent a place of his own, and then he let the business come to him.

Those who had been paupers were now kings in the strange new world that he had awoken in. He had been spat upon in the streets and looked down on by everyone, and now he had the rich and the beautiful courting him for attention. The attention may only have been for the things that he could offer them, but in his experience of the world, everyone wanted something from you, so he may as well enjoy it.

By the time Hans came to join him in Hanover, he had himself set up in a lavishly decorated single-bedroom apartment with all the modern conveniences. The young man did not need to fear boredom, either, as the local nightlife, which had sprung into existence fully formed from the ashes of Germany's imperial dreams, was more than accepting of both homosexual relationships and criminals like them. In fact, most of the local cabaret bars serving bootlegged liquor were buying it through Fritz and his connections. He could get a table in any restaurant and a seat in any nightclub. He had gone from a pariah to a hot property so quickly that it made his head spin.

Still, the small cut that he was receiving in exchange for his work facilitating trades like that was not enough to live on. Instead, he had dug deep into his old business research and contacted local farms about their meat. Since food was still rationed, the farmers had very little opportunity to turn a profit, no matter how good their product was, receiving a flat rate, by weight, for all the meat that they turned over. Through Fritz, they suddenly had an alternate revenue stream. Selling their highest quality meat to him for significantly more than the government stipend and allowing him to hike up the price even higher before selling it on the black market. To his mind, it was a win-win. The rich got their meat, the farmers got their pay, and if the government didn't have quite enough pork to fill out the sausage ration, that was hardly his concern, was it? Fritz was back in the game, and he was winning, truly winning, for the first time in his life. He was more of a success than his father had ever been, and he'd done it all by himself, with no inheritance stolen from a wife, no old union buddies hooking him up with the best jobs going, he was a self-made man. And if he'd made himself into something that would have made his father sick to the stomach just to look at him, then all the better.

Of course, with his newfound success came a return of police attention. He knew that it was only a matter of time before they took an interest in his dealings, most of the cops that had survived the war would know him on sight and know that he was up to no good. So, he returned to his old haunt, Hanover Central Station, and got himself caught up as quickly as possible. Filing away details on the comings and goings, learning who the new movers and shakers were, and even finding the perfect way to reintroduce himself to the local constabulary. When he spotted that a newly arrived traveller was in possession of forged travel documents, he performed a citizen's arrest and subsequently frog-marched the man to the very same police station where he himself had been booked half a decade before.

From then on, he was an almost daily visitor to the police station, strolling in as though he owned the place, tipping his hat to the sergeant on desk duty and letting himself in to see if there were any cases that he could help with. Despite his effete mannerisms, he smoked rough cigars, just like most of the older policemen, and when it became apparent that he was willing to share, he went from being a fixture of the station to being an old friend for many of them. Even men who'd arrested him many times through the years would have gladly bought him a drink in those days. Once again, it was as though the whole world had been turned on its head, and everything that had once made sense was nonsense.

What should have been the one constant in Fritz's life, the one thing that would have kept him on steady ground, was the man that he had bound his life to. The sweet boy that he had found in prison and brought out of destitution to live a life of luxury. Yet Hans was rarely around, even once he had officially moved to Hanover, and into Fritz's apartment. Perhaps he was not as comfortable as Fritz when it came to living openly as a homosexual. Perhaps the sole double bed in the apartment had put him off the idea of staying there every night. Most likely though, it was simply a matter of old habits dying hard. He had been a street rat and pimp long before Fritz met him, and that kind of criminal history was a hard thing to shake. Just as Fritz was slipping back into his old criminal ways, so too was Hans, though with markedly less success than his lover.

These long periods of absence would understandably have hurt Fritz's feelings. He likely began to fear that the young man he'd ensnared wasn't going to come back to him at all. That he'd found another lover to take care of him. That what had been good enough for prison wasn't good enough now that they were out here in the real world where people could see them. The fact that Hans was ostensibly heterosexual outside of their highly transactional relationship also poured fuel on the fire of his doubts. He did not only need to compete with all of the other gay men of Hanover for the attention of his young lover but with every woman too. Women who could provide the little pimp with both an outwardly normal life in comparison to what Fritz could, but also a source of steady income when he prostituted them.

As the power disparity in their relationship became increasingly marked, the few demands that Fritz made upon his younger lover became even fewer, and the things that he offered became even more bountiful. Hans was, of course, delighted with this change, in no small part because it meant he didn't have to subject himself to Fritz's ever-amorous attentions. It was the best of both worlds for him, he got all the benefits of his relationship with Fritz while finding his own satisfaction elsewhere. For Fritz, however, this presented a serious problem. He no longer had a sexual outlet.

This was not the first time that he had found himself in this situation, and as always, he was more than willing to mix work with pleasure. The central station had always provided him with young men, disconnected from their friends and family, trying to start a new life in the aftermath of the war. Since leaving prison, however, he had only been using them in a non-carnal manner, bilking them out of money, passing them along to whichever criminal enterprise might have a use for them. Now he began making use of them in other ways.

With his frustrations over his relationship with Hans mounting, he was now also developing a genuine terror of what would happen if they were parted by another prison sentence. Without his constant presence, he did not doubt that Hans would move on with his life and find someone else to rely on. He could not go back to jail. This meant that if he were to take another lover, the way that he used to, then he would need to ensure that they could not go and make a complaint to the police about his molestation. Relying upon their fear of being outed as a participant in a sexual relationship with another man was no longer sufficient.

The dichotomy of Fritz Haarmann's psyche was that he could coldly calculate things like this, yet the expression of these plans came in the form of passionate outbursts. Almost as though all of his careful planning and philosophising were only there to justify the things that he already wanted to do but refused to acknowledge, even to himself. Certainly, he had been cut off from his father's fortune and influence as well as from his wife and children, but escaping both those situations had always been what he'd fundamentally desired, as evidenced by his flight to the army over and over again. Who he was at his core had never been changed by his circumstances, it had only been repressed or let loose depending upon what he felt he could justify to others and to himself. He may have been free from his father looking over his shoulder and judging his every action, but the voice inside of his head that sounded so like Olle was still there, and he was still making excuses to it for everything that he wanted, and everything that he did. He may have ascribed it to caution, or a fear of society's reactions, but by this point, he was already so far beyond the boundary of what was acceptable to society that it was almost comical that he might still be fearful. As though the neighbours were going to gossip about him and ruin his chances at a great career when he was a black-market butcher, police informant, and ex-convict with a gay lover.

The first time that he took one of his new lovers is not known but the first official record began with Friedel Rothe.

Rothe was a seventeen-year-old boy, a resident of Hanover returning from elsewhere in the country when he caught Fritz's attention at the station. For all that Fritz was considered something of a degenerate by the older people of the city, the younger generation had something resembling respect for the man. They were more progressive in terms of accepting his sexuality and viewed him as something of a minor celebrity thanks to the way that he was treated in the bars and cabarets that they frequented. According to the testimony of his friends, Friedel was quite taken with Fritz, enjoying his company, and more or less allowing himself to be seduced by the older man, culminating in the two of them departing from the bar to return to Fritz's apartment. It was the last time that the boy was seen alive.

From the bar, Fritz and the giggling young man made their way back to his apartment. Fritz had spent several hours plying the young man with bootleg liquor and had promised more of the same in abundance back at his home, though both of them knew from the outset that this was simply an excuse for them to go there. Once the door was locked behind them,

Fritz let the pretence slip away, the two of them kissed awkwardly for a few moments as they stumbled their way through to the bedroom, but then the reality of what was about to happen seemed to sink in for the teenager. Fritz had no such hesitation, physically stripping the clothes off the boy as he continued to force him backwards into the room, towards the bed. Despite his protests and struggles, Fritz managed to strip him down to his undergarments without any damage to the outfit, something that was important to its resale value. But from there on, it seemed that anything resembling rational thought had escaped Fritz's mind.

When the back of Friedel's knees hit the bed and he toppled back, all of the bigger older man's weight upon him, he realised that no matter what happened next it would be entirely outside of his control. Even as Fritz kissed down the side of his neck, and his mouth was freed to beg him to stop, the uselessness of such begging became abundantly clear. Fritz's eyes were glazed over, whether with lust or liquor, the thinking part of him was no longer in control. He had become a creature of instinct, dragging in heady breaths of the teenager's scent even as he mouthed his way down across the pale taut skin of the boy's collarbone and to his chest.

Through his lips, Fritz could feel a heartbeat. Through his fingertips, where they dug into the boy's hips, he could feel the warmth of the living, struggling body beneath him. It was the most alive that he had felt in months, years, perhaps his whole life. Not that he was even vaguely aware of that in the moment. Not when his whole body, usually silenced and ignored, came alive at the touch of another human being. There was a pot of grease on the bedside table, and he reached for it without breaking away from the boy, without giving him a moment's respite to gather his thoughts or his strength. There would be none of that. He had him now, and he was never ever going to let him go. This was a boy who could not go wandering, one that could never betray him or lose interest. This was the perfect, sweet boy that he'd always wanted for himself through all the hard years. He would not ever let him go.

As he tried to restrain the boy and work his blunt, greased-up fingers inside him at the same time, Friedel's struggles became all the more frantic. With one hand occupied, and an awkward angle preventing him from bringing the rest of his weight to bear, Fritz couldn't keep him under control. In his fear at the intrusion into his body, the boy had begun to shout, to call out for help. Fritz could not allow that.

He pressed back down on top of him, abandoning the work of his hands to focus on the more pressing problem. The boy tried to buck him off, but he just didn't have the strength or the coordination in his drunken, breathless state. Fritz pressed a kiss to Friedel's soft underbelly, gnashing his teeth, hoping that the sharp prick would still the boy, but it just made him all the more afraid and frantic. He kissed his way up across his chest, ignoring the clumsy blows coming down on his back and shoulders. Making his way further and further toward the source of all the damnable noise.

The boy squealed. He screamed. He called out for help. Even the gentle kisses that Fritz was pressing into the side of his neck, which had worked so well to silence him in the beginning were no longer working. He bowed his back off the bed, trying once more to throw Fritz off, throwing back his head. Exposing his throat.

Without even thinking about what he was doing, following some instinct deeply embedded in the predatory part of his brain, Fritz brought his mouth back down onto the centre of the boy's throat, and he bit down.

There was no soft and giving flesh there. Just the hard gristle of the boy's Adam's apple. What Fritz thought of as his voicebox. If it could be squeezed shut, then the noise would stop. The screaming, the flailing, he could make it all stop if he just bit down a little harder. When his teeth tore through skin, Fritz didn't even notice, when they ground through the cartilage and closed shut, he still didn't stop. Biting until his own teeth ached with the pressure. It was only when the boy went completely silent and still that he pushed himself back up off the boy to take in what he had done, jaw still locked shut and the throbbing meat still heavy on his tongue.

Blood ran down Fritz's chin. It gushed from the open wound of the boy's neck. Pulsing out in time to the thundering of his heart. His eyes were still wide and terrified. It was the greatest rush that Fritz had ever felt in his life. Making this perfect boy even more perfect in his stillness and compliance.

As Friedel went through his death throes, soaking the bedding and mattress through with his lifeblood, Fritz went back to work with lubricant and fingers, forcing the boy's unresisting legs up and then sliding himself inside.

He raped the boy as he lay dying, hammering flesh into slowly cooling flesh until finally, he was satisfied. His own head thrown back. His own back arching.

It was only after the bright white light of his orgasm had passed that Fritz came back to himself and saw clearly what he had done.

There was a dead body lying in his bed. There was blood everywhere. He had killed the boy to make him silent. He had planned to kill the boy to make him silent. No matter what the nagging voice in the back of his head had to say about the morality of murder, the practical part of him could not help but be pleased that it had been so easily achieved. He had been picturing some awful scenario in which after he had found his satisfaction, he would have had to go for one of the knives he had hidden in the drawers by his bed and make a fateful cut. That would have felt more like cold-blooded murder to Fritz. This just felt like it was a part of his lovemaking.

The body had stopped bleeding. All spasmodic movement finally stilled. As Fritz pulled out of the corpse, he stared down and could not contain his giggling.

Lovemaking.

This was what his love had made.

He let his body cool, let the body beneath him cool, let all of the passion drain from him slowly so that his thoughts once again became clear. There was now a dead body in his apartment and it could not remain there. The smell would bring attention, if nothing else. And given that avoiding unwanted attention had been his stated purpose in killing his young lover, that would be counterproductive. He carefully stripped out of his blood-soaked clothes, regretting that he had not thought to remove them all in the run-up to his killing. He was about to begin cleaning up the room and himself when he realised that it would be a wasted effort until the body was removed. Opening his mouth, at last, he let the hunk of meat that had been resting on his tongue throughout the last few minutes drop and land on the boy's limp form. Perhaps he should have felt some disgust at having had human flesh in his mouth, but he had been working as a black-market butcher for so long now that to him, meat was meat.

Those were the words that echoed in his head as he pondered the best way to dispose of a full-grown man. Meat was meat. He went and fetched his butchering tools and let his perspective shift. First, he would skin the animal, then remove the organs and set them aside. Finally, he would butcher the meat from the bones. The bones, he realised, would be the only real dilemma in terms of disposal. He could break down the organs to the point that they were unrecognisable, feed them to stray dogs or simply dump them out somewhere and let decay take its course. The meat... he already had established buyers for any meat that he happened to come by, and any excess could be dealt with in the same way as the organs. The bones though, even if he smashed them apart, would be recognisable. He needed to dispose of them somewhere easily accessible yet where they would never be found.

Starting with decapitation, he broke down the corpse into its component parts as he had planned. The whole room still reeked like a slaughterhouse, but he had butchered here before, and he knew that it would disperse with time. To his mind, the skull was the most easily recognisable part of the human body and the part that he would most certainly be arrested for carting around, while the rest could probably be passed off as some other animal. Rather than run the risk of being caught with it, he tied up the head of Friedel Rothe in some cheesecloth and hid it behind his stovepipe. That would suffice, at least for now.

With that done, he sealed up all of the good meat in butcher's paper and bagged the organs that he did not think that he could dice and sell. He took the bones and organs for an evening stroll to Stoekner Cemetery where he set about burying them. It was arduous work for a man who was no longer accustomed to heavy physical labour, and he decided then and there that he would need a better system for disposal in the future, as this was exhausting.

Over the next few days, Rothe's absence was noted, both by his friends and his family. He was reported to the police as a missing person, and within a few short interviews, they were able to narrow down their list of suspects to one. Fritz Haarmann. He had been seen openly canoodling with the boy, he was a known homosexual with a record of abducting young men to indulge his sexual proclivities, and in truth, most of the police suspected that if they were to go knocking on his door, they would find the two of them in an ongoing tryst that the Rothe boy was too embarrassed to leave given how brazenly he'd given himself over to Haarmann. This presented a problem for the police. Knowing that Fritz was a homosexual and catching him in the act were two entirely different legal propositions. They could ignore his homosexuality forever so long as they never saw it happening, but if they went to his apartment and found the boy there with him, they would have no choice but to arrest him. Something that they were obviously loath to do, given his value as an informant.

During those days, Fritz went about his usual routine, visiting the train station, selling off his black-market meat to the usual buyers and dropping into the police station to chat with all of his usual friends and contacts. All of whom were aware that he was currently under investigation for the abduction and corruption of a young man, but none of whom were willing to sour their relationship with him, or spoil the investigation, unless they absolutely had to.

If left to their own devices, likely, the police would simply have let the matter lie, assume that the boy had left town to avoid the new reputation that he'd gained, and write him off as yet another run-away in a city that seemed to be teeming with them. But Rothe's family were not so willing to let bygones be bygones. They hounded the police, even contacting local papers about their lack of action, until finally with their hand forced, they went to raid Fritz Haarmann's apartment.

Every officer attending knew the man and was reluctant to destroy the tentative trust between informant and officer. They were all hoping and praying that they would break down the door and discover that Rothe had long since departed and they would not have to pursue this line of investigation further. They would not be so lucky, nor would Fritz.

When they came bursting into the apartment in an explosion of motion, Fritz froze in place as though he was paralyzed. As did the naked teenage boy that he was entangled with on the bed.

There was no way to talk their way out of this, no way to avoid the inevitable outcome for them all. With any other crime, they may have been apologetic as they arrested Fritz after catching him in the act but for the majority of the strictly conservative police force, disgust was vying with their irritation that Haarmann had put them in this situation to begin with, thanks to his inclinations. The boy was sent on his way as soon as he'd struggled back into his clothes, once his statement had been taken, and Fritz was hauled off to jail to await trial.

A cursory glance over the apartment showed clear evidence of butchery having taken place there, but this was not considered to be suspicious, given that he was a known black-market trader, and half the police force had probably relied upon him for a nice cut of meat on more than one occasion. If their examination had been more than cursory; if they had treated Fritz like he was a real suspect in the disappearance of Friedel Rothe, and explored every inch of the apartment, they would have found the boy's decapitated head was still stored behind the stovepipe.

The hunt for Rothe went cold after that, the family were partially satisfied to see that Fritz was being sent to jail on related charges, but they still had no idea what had become of their son, gradually coming to believe in the police narrative that he had run away from home rather than face the repercussions of his dalliance with the older gay man. This was exacerbated by a letter that they received in the post, confirming in Friedel's handwriting that he was running away from home and would not return until his mother 'was nice again.' Something that he had penned and posted before he had even crossed paths with Fritz Haarmann. A stroke of luck for Fritz. One of many, given everything that could have gone wrong.

For Fritz, the timing of the raid had been impeccable. If the police had arrived only a few minutes later, they likely would have found him raping a teen boy's corpse, and he could not imagine that the court would be handing him down a slap on the wrist for that. While he was sentenced to serve nine months in prison, he was able to defer his confinement, helped in no small part by the political upheaval that was taking place in Germany at the time. It was during this upheaval that the emperor and his family fled and a republic was established with the express intention of never leading the German people so badly astray as their royal leaders had done. For those living on the ground floor of society, it meant very little in practical terms. For those that operated the bureaucracy of the country, however, it ushered in a period of great turmoil with new laws and statutes being rushed in to replace the old ones. It was unfortunate for Fritz that he had been arrested before this period in September of 1918. He likely would have seen more lenient sentencing as the old imperial laws regarding sexual conduct were also overturned, and many past offences were scrubbed from criminal records. At least the deferment of his sentence allowed Fritz the time necessary to clear his apartment of any incriminating evidence, sell off all of the goods that he was meant to fence, and accumulate a small nest egg to pass on to Hans so that the boy would not struggle in his absence.

When the time came, and Fritz turned himself in to the police, Hans was left homeless and directionless. The money that Fritz had left him was soon spent on hotel rooms and liquor, and before a third of Haarmann's sentence was complete, Hans was homeless. He slept mostly on the benches at the train station in the months that followed.

It appeared that the once feral boy that Fritz had taken into his home had become somewhat domesticated and was no longer suited to life in the wild. This likely came as something of a surprise to Hans, too. Throughout their relationship, he had frequently walked out on Fritz, claiming that he would manage just fine without the older man's support, and he had thoroughly believed it, too. Waiting for Fritz to come grovelling and begging for him to return to their shared home and their shared bed. Now, with how hard it was to make ends meet for everyone, he discovered that the abundant resources that he had once relied upon to pay his way had dried up. He was no longer one of the few disenfranchised youths preying upon the wealthy and the comfortable, he was one of the hundreds of such men who had come home from war to find the rug pulled out from under their whole existence.

Despite the limited funds he managed to wheedle out of mutual acquaintances, he still spent some of it making the trip out to the prison to visit with Fritz.

All the fears that had plagued Fritz regarding the longevity of their relationship vanished in those moments. He was too blinded by sentiment to realise that his young companion had finally realised just how much of his comfort he owed to Fritz's care. Instead, he completely believed that the irregular visits were a clear sign that his love for the younger man was reciprocated. That on his release from prison, they would be reunited, and live together like a couple, instead of sporadically drifting through one another's orbits.

If that was what it took for Hans to avoid having to pay his way, then he was willing to make that compromise.

The Butcher of Hanover

With his release in the autumn of 1920, Fritz stepped right back into the same routines that he had followed before. Hans met him from the train station, and the two of them set about finding some accommodation for themselves, lodging in the suburban home of a married couple until Haarmann's criminal empire, or rather, republic, could regain its footing. Much of the post-war rationing was still in place, allowing him to resume his trade in black-market meat, but many of the other restrictions that had been placed upon the German people by its petulant nobility were beginning to fade. Trade had been opened up with neighbouring countries, and with the regime change came a renewed willingness to do business with Germany. On the one hand, this was a wonderful development for the average German who could now enjoy a slightly higher quality of life, but it was terrible news for the war-profiteering smugglers who had made their living by bringing the goods that could not be gotten through legitimate means into the country. Many of Fritz's business connections had dried up. Those that hadn't were now transitioning from dealing in goods which previously were merely considered morally reprehensible to dealing in goods which had recently become outrightly illegal in the new political climate.

This of course meant that a great many of them now had to deal with a fence for the first time in their lives, and as luck would have it, the gentleman who had been helping to facilitate their illegal trade up until that point happened to be one of the city's most notorious. Of course, much had changed in the nine months that he was away, and he had to rapidly catch up with many of his old acquaintances and make a great many new ones to boot. What he needed was a quick and condensed update on criminal activity within the city, so that is precisely what he went looking for. Strolling into the police station as though the men there had not been responsible for his arrest.

At first, the police were taken aback, having expected there to be at least some degree of bad blood between them and their perverse informant, but it seemed that he felt nothing of the kind. Walking in as though he owned the place and sitting down with the detectives to catch up as though he had been on holiday rather than imprisoned.

Within a few hours, rather than a few days, he had heard about all of the biggest robberies and burglaries to occur in the city and caught the names of those who were presumed responsible. A laundry list of new clients for him to seek out and offer representation to.

In turn, when he returned to the police station the following day after reaching out to all of these new premier thieves, he had a list of addresses to turn over. Those addresses just happened to be for all those who had refused to do business with him. It was a golden haul for the police and reaffirmed Fritz's role as a valued informant while also removing all competition from the market in one fell swoop. It could not have worked out better for him if it had been planned that way.

As a result of this quid pro quo, he was brought entirely back within the confidence of the police and given free rein to tour the station as he once had. This in turn provided fresh opportunities for him, because here he could find those teenage runaways and vagrants who lacked the street smarts to survive on their own in Hanover without attracting the attention of the police. A shallow dating pool for a man like him, but shallow in the same way that fish in a barrel swim in shallow waters. On more than one occasion he offered room and board to one of these foolish young wastrels, and by the time anyone was aware that they had gone missing from the police station, they had also gone missing from the streets, and from the entire city.

This was hardly cause for concern for the police. It was quite the opposite. In his way, Fritz was clearing the streets of the homeless and disaffected, and reducing the amount of paperwork that the police had to file every day. It was not as though these young men who went missing had families that were going to come looking for them. Fritz had learned his lessons from his last victim, and he had no intention of becoming the subject of another 'witch hunt' just because he happened to have been seen with a young man shortly before he went missing.

Throughout all of this, Hans became aware of what Fritz was doing.

The exact date that he became aware is unclear, but at some point, he walked into the apartment that they had been sharing since being forcibly evicted from their boarding house and found Fritz in the midst of disposing of a body. Suddenly, the source of all the gifts of clothing that he had been receiving from Fritz became clear. Also clear was the reason he so often had to spend an evening sewing buttons back onto said shirts. Fritz stayed very still for a moment as his young lover watched him, the cheeks of his moon-shaped face flushed with arousal and exertion. He did not say anything, did not offer up any excuse or denial of what the boy was seeing. He simply waited to see if Hans would still accept him now that the truth was out. Hans' eyes were drawn away from the dead boy where he lay, throat torn out by Fritz's 'love bite' to the tools of the butcher's trade that were already arrayed across the bloodstained floor. Pieces of the puzzle began clicking into place, and when understanding finally arrived, he was very careful in how he spoke.

All this time, he had treated the older man as something of a harmless joke. That now came to an end. He did not abruptly develop a sense of respect for his lover, you could not break the habit of so many years that swiftly. But he could recognise that he had blundered into something very, very dangerous and took to the streets. For those brief moments when he locked eyes with Fritz before he fled, he saw the true face of evil. Not some dark eyes devoid of emotion, or some deranged glare, but the very same expression that Fritz wore upon his face every day. Nothing was changed by the dead boy in his hands. Fritz worked that meat the same as he did any other. He went through the motions of slaughter in the same way that a normal man would buff his shoes. The terror was not in the bizarreness of the situation, but in its absolute mundanity. For Fritz, this was just another day.

If the gormless smile and adoration shining out of Fritz's eyes had been absent, then everything might have been so much simpler for Hans. He could have cut all ties, could have even gone so far as to report the crime if it became necessary to keep Fritz away from him, but the look on Fritz's face, even when he was caught in the act, was one of joy to be seeing Hans again. Even with everything else that was happening, he only had eyes for Hans.

He could still work with this. Men kept dogs as pets, and a dog could tear out your throat. The trick would be to tame this wild hound, to train him to bark and bite only as he was commanded. But how much more valuable was a dog with some fight in it, than some useless lump that just lay around all day wanting its belly scratched. The possibilities seemed to blossom out in front of Hans. Where other men might have been afraid, he still remained confident in his ability to control the monster that he had found himself bound to. The fact that the young man that he had just seen Fritz murdering looked so much like him was surely a coincidence. Nothing to worry about.

Hans pushed his fears aside and then began calculating the profit in this whole murderous enterprise. There would be the money in the boys' wallets, the sale of the meat, if Fritz could be convinced to pass it off as ground pork, the resale value of the clothes on their back, and any jewellery the little punks happened to be wearing when they ran away from home to seek a better life in the big city. The possibilities were endless. Because all the various and somewhat disorganised criminal enterprises were currently enjoying a perpetual flow of business that was difficult to keep up with, and because there was little to no competition for that business, there was very little call for assassination in the underworld of Hanover during the Weimer Republic era, but the idea that Fritz could be wielded as a blunt instrument to threaten people was quite appealing. It wouldn't work, of course, Fritz still had the affect of a comedically effeminate homosexual, which simply was not intimidating to German men. The only way that anyone could possibly know just how dangerous Fritz was would be to show him in action, giving others leverage over Fritz that they could use to manipulate him to their own ends. Unacceptable to Hans, who may not have had any real love or even affection for the man, but who was still extremely jealous of his attention or loyalties being split.

Only one person would control Fritz, and that was him. Not the police, not other criminals, not anyone. All that he had to do was play it sweet for a while longer. Keep Fritz hooked on the line instead of dangling at arms-length all the time. He could manage that. Especially if the extra discomfort he'd have to tolerate came with all the extra cash that Fritz was going to be taking from the boys.

By the time he had calmed himself and come home, Fritz was finished cleaning up. The clothes from the dead man still lay neatly folded on a chair, the air still held the metallic tang of blood. But whatever other traces of the deceased remained within their shared apartment could no longer be seen. Neither man wanted to be the first to broach the subject, worrying just how far the other might run if pressed, but then again, neither man was willing to back down. As Hans approached his old lover, it was with the kind of watchful apprehension normally only seen in zoo keepers entering the enclosure of a beast they knew to be friendly but was nonetheless capable of tearing them apart. For Fritz's part, he stayed as still as he possibly could, worried that the slightest movement might startle Hans into running.

When they finally came together, it was not with words that things were settled, but by touch. Hans brought up a hand to cradle Fritz's cheek. Fritz wrapped his arms around his beloved boy. Their lips touched, ever so gently. Like it was a formality. Like it was their wedding day and they were vowing their unconditional acceptance of each other for all to see.

For Hans, the dead man in his bed might have been the greatest revelation of the day, but for Fritz, it was this moment. He had been seen for who he really was, what he really was, and Hans was still accepting him. Still offering him everything that he'd always wanted. All the weight of shame that had been bearing down on Fritz from the first moment that he had memories was suddenly lifted. The voice of his father in the back of his head, always damning him, always demanding justification or grovelling apologies, fell silent. He was known, and he was loved, for who he was. He did not need to hide anymore. He did not need to fear anymore. He was not an idiot, he still realised that discretion would be necessary for him to navigate a world that was fundamentally hostile to his nature and his interests, but there was now some small solace in this world. A beautiful boy, who was just like his mother. A boy who could fully grasp that all the wonderful things inside of him were made up of twisted parts, but that their components did not make the whole less beautiful, but all the more wonderous for it. Anyone could make a piece of art with the right brushes and paints, but to make it with blade and blood, that took true talent.

It was about this time that the two of them moved into a new apartment on the ground floor of 8 Neue Straße. The building was already densely populated with renters, and the ground floor flat wasn't really considered to be suitable for human habitation. As such, Fritz got a very good deal on the place, telling his new landlady that he meant only to use it for storage for his various business ventures. Once he had the keys, it took very little time for Fritz to haul all his belongings and furniture over from his last apartment or to call in some favours from various people with the necessary connections to help him incorporate the luxury touches he'd always wanted to treat Hans to. All stolen furniture and goods, of course. But goods that Fritz would claim he meant to sell for his clients while making good use of them in the meantime.

This created a base of operations for Fritz that the police were not immediately aware of. One where he could conduct his business without risk of them showing up unexpectedly. It gave him back control over their relationship. He was no longer at their beck and call, he had to be treated with a degree of respect. This was the chastisement that the police of Hanover had long been expecting from him, but it was subtle enough that it could all too easily be passed off as a misunderstanding so that no feelings need be hurt.

With all the extra space in the new apartment, Fritz's criminal enterprises flourished. He was a much more effective fence now that he had a small warehouse in which to store those stolen goods which passed into his care, and he was a more effective butcher now that he had a dedicated space to ply that craft. Only he and Hans truly knew what that craft entailed, but that did not mean that they held themselves in isolation. Quite the opposite. With the new space, and a newfound ability to sequester the less savoury elements of their lifestyle, Fritz and Hans began entertaining guests in their Neue Straße apartment. They proudly offered home-cooked meals with the finest, unrationed ingredients, cocktails and more. It became a happening hub of activity within the city. A place that the regular low-lives of Hanover hoped they might someday be invited to.

Hans began inviting over girlfriends, and their friends, under the guise of double dating with Fritz, and while everyone cottoned onto the joke fairly early in the evening, any sting that Fritz's 'date' might have felt tended to be fairly thoroughly soothed with his kind words, attention, and no small amount of wine.

Given what is known of Fritz's psyche, it would have been reasonable to assume that he would have flown into some sort of jealous rage at the sight of Hans with a female companion. However, this did not seem to be the case. If anything, he seemed to actively encourage the younger man's conquests and befriended many of the young women that were pursuing him. He took on the persona of a sort of eccentric uncle to the young man, a benefactor who was seeking for his beneficiary to receive only the best in life. When the girls Hans brought around weren't to his liking, he certainly made that known, but it seemed to be more in the manner of a friend who was overly involved in the youngster's life, particularly given the outright praise that he offered up some of the others.

In turn, he swiftly realised that he could bring his own 'dates' to these dinner parties, under the guise of setting them up with friends of Hans'. The mixed group and jovial setting lulled these boys into a false sense of security that would persist until the early hours of the morning when Hans departed with his young lady, Fritz offered to put the youngster up until morning, and nature took its course. The assumption being that we are limiting our understanding of "nature" to those apex predators who pounce upon their prey and tear out their throats. What followed those moments tended to be the sort of thing that is described as categorically unnatural.

On the 12th of February 1923, Fritz encountered a young pianist by the name of Fritz Franke from Berlin, who was travelling to Hanover in search of work. The boy was sixteen years old, having barely escaped being drafted for the Great War, and was as moon-faced and gullible as visitors to the city came.

Given that he had no stated destination or any place to sleep that night, the elder Fritz offered up his apartment. He was having a dinner party for some of the city's up-and-comers, and he was sure that they would be delighted to meet a talented young man like Fritz Franke.

At first, the boy was understandably apprehensive, but before long, Hans and his lady-friends arrived and the young pianist found himself caught up in the glitz and glamour of their lives, heading out of the train station and straight along the Neue Straße to where dinner awaited.

The evening's entertainment, as it turned out, was not going to be provided by him as he feared. There wasn't even a piano in Fritz's apartment. Or if there was, it was buried under his 'antique collection.' Rather, it seemed that their host with his queer little mannerisms and sharp tongue was to be the font of merriment for everyone involved. Fritz Franke had never seen a man who was so comfortable in himself, so willing to let others make a mockery of him without feeling the sting of their words. It was remarkable how little care Haarmann had for the opinion of others. In his position, Franke would have been wincing and blushing, not making lewd jokes about his own proclivities. The boy was not some country rube, he had grown up in Berlin and thought that he'd always lived a fairly cosmopolitan life, but the way that this lot carried on put the rebels of home to shame. The flirtation between them would have been racy even if they had respected gender lines, but the fact that everyone at the table expressed interest in him, in one way or another, was almost too much for his young mind to comprehend. He felt as though he had been offered a dry beef sandwich and then arrived at dinner to discover a smorgasbord on offer instead.

His ego began to flourish under the attention, and soon he was joking back and forth with the rest of them, admittedly with somewhat less success due to his unfamiliarity with some of the coarse subject matter. He even managed to squeeze in a few jibes at his host, causing an eruption of laughter and leading him to make more attempts at the same, sending undeniably rude comments in the direction of Hans.

For a moment the table stilled as they waited to see just how the young pimp's temper would flare, and whether it would be amusingly dramatic, but instead, Hans just smiled and settled back with his drink. His date leaned in close to enquire why he was just taking such an insult without defending himself and he replied, 'That boy is going to be run over tomorrow.'

His current paramour looked askance at him, trying to understand what he meant. It was unclear whether he was making one of his usual veiled threats, making some grand philosophical statement about how short life was, or whether he knew with some certainty that something bad was going to happen to the younger Fritz. During the dinner party, she had no opportunity to pry further, and by the end of the night when they were staggering back to her rooms, leaving little Fritz Franke to sleep off the drink on their gracious host's living room floor, they too had imbibed so much alcohol as to render any attempts at coherent thought moot.

She probably wouldn't have even remembered the odd comment at all come morning, were it not for the fact that she and Hans were meeting up with Fritz and some other friends the next day for an early lunch. The rest of their group arrived, but she made sure to keep a pair of seats free for Fritz and his identically named guest, so she was taken aback to discover that the boy was not with Fritz when he showed up, late as usual. She asked after him and was brushed off with the excuse that he had caught an early train home to Berlin. This made no sense at all. The boy had spoken at length about his plans to seek employment in Hanover, the possibility of teaching the piano to the children of well-off families, or a place in one of the cabaret bars. Nothing in his words or demeanour had given any hint that he was so overwrought with homesickness that he meant to flee back to cling to his mother's apron strings the very moment that the sun rose.

Nothing about his sudden departure made sense, but Hans seemed to accept it as though it were nothing. As if he already knew the truth. As if he knew what had happened to the boy before it had even happened.

The others chatted and laughed and ate, but she felt numb. That little boy, barely old enough to shave had been sat across from her the night before, having the time of his life, chatting and laughing and eating, just like all of them were right now. But he was not here now. She couldn't say with any certainty what had happened to him. Whether he had some falling out with Fritz and they went their separate ways, or the older man pressured him into some situation that had made him so uncomfortable that he had to flee. She did not know what might have run him over as Hans had predicted, or how Hans could possibly have foreseen such a thing. Asking Hans about it repeatedly after lunch only served to make his temper flare and spoil the rest of their day. He left her back at home and went off to go about his other business, which she had no doubt involved the seduction of other women. It was as harsh a rebuff as she'd ever received from him. A clear message to leave it alone. And she did. There was no point in causing trouble in her life over what had befallen some Berliner who was essentially a stranger. They may have shared dinner, but there was no bond between them, and if Fritz had come onto him and scared him off, or laid hands on him and made him too ashamed to show his face anymore, that was no business of hers. The world was a hard place, especially for runaways. She knew that herself all too well, and she wasn't willing to throw away the things that made her life easier out of fear for some boy she had only just met.

Hans was, in fact, not going romancing that afternoon. Quite the contrary. Instead, he went to Fritz's apartment and let himself in. He did have a key, after all. Fritz would have had him living there full-time if Hans allowed it.

Inside the apartment, it was exactly as he had expected to find it. All was quiet and still. He strolled without caution to the workspace, where he caught the familiar aroma of slaughter hanging in the air. The charnel house reek of blood, bowels and decay. Opening the door, he found Fritz still at his work, stripped to the waist, body slicked with sweat and grime. He just stood there and watched him work, feeling something twisting in his own guts as he watched the little pianist's carcass be unravelled. Something that might have been admiration, or maybe even attraction. Eventually, Fritz seemed to come out of that fugue state that took him when he was hard at his butchery, and he glanced up to see his young lover standing there, watching him carve up last night's lover. Hans spoke softly, voice trembling with this strange new emotion that had taken hold of him, 'When should I come back?'

And there, on the blood-streaked face of the murderer, was bound to appear the same soppy smile that he saw every time he showed any hint of kindness or affection. As gormless as it had ever been. Fritz told him it would be a few hours until he was done, but he was welcome to stay and have a browse through the dead man's luggage to see if there was anything that he wanted.

Squeamish as he might have been, Hans was still himself. He wouldn't turn down an opportunity like that. And he was still wearing the dead boy's clothes when he fell into bed with Fritz that night. All the pretence that he didn't want Fritz was thrown aside as his rough lips played across Hans' throat.

The Year of Blood

Hans went from being an accessory after the fact, to being intimately involved in Fritz's murders from that point on. He would spot pretty young boys and point them out to Fritz, even chatting with them to make the procurement all the easier. Setting them at ease in a way that Fritz himself could never quite manage, what with his oddness and age difference. Some of these boys, Hans would pick out of convenience, because he didn't feel inclined to give himself over to Fritz's pleasures that night. Others he picked out of jealousy, either because they had nicer clothes than him that he coveted or because he didn't like the way that Fritz was treating them like equals. They were not equals, they were marks, they were prey, they shouldn't be spoken to with affection, except to the point that they were snared. His ambivalence about his lover killed so many; he did not want Fritz for himself, but neither did he want anyone else to have him. On the surface, he always maintained the impression of love for Fritz, so that he never became at risk of becoming another one of his victims, but internally he was torn between many conflicting emotions about his relationship with the older man.

On March 20th 1923, Wilhelm Schulze, an apprentice writer, came to the city of Hanover to pursue a new master, having found his previous employer to be ill-tempered. He was seventeen years old and bore exactly the looks that had drawn Fritz to Hans in the beginning. He was seen disembarking the train at Hanover Central Station where Fritz lurked as always, but afterwards, he simply vanished from sight. There was no trace of him to be found anywhere, no witnesses that could place his movements after stepping off the train. It was as though the platform had opened up and swallowed him whole. The next day, Hans was strutting around town in a new suit that looked like it could have been tailored for him. Waving around a new silk handkerchief. Looking more like a dandy than the bottom-feeder that he was.

Three days later, Roland Huch, a fifteen-year-old student vanished in exactly the same way. Hans was not seen wearing the boy's clothes, but acquaintances of Fritz who were on the shorter side soon purchased them. None of these victims was particularly profitable, but for Fritz, the financial aspects of his crimes were beginning to feel less and less important. He had found an outlet for all of his emotions, the wild tangle of rage and sexual repression that had always characterised his inner self was finally unleashed, and he felt alive in a way that he hadn’t known that he could.

A few days later, 18-year-old Hans Sonnerfeld, a runaway who had come to Hanover to escape his oppressive parents found himself as a part of Fritz’s entourage touring the cabarets and then returning to the man’s apartment for drinks and a late dinner. Come morning, no sign of him could be found at all. The dirty dishes were cleaned, the wine bottles tossed away. With all the unwanted refuse disposed of, it was as though the good times the night before had never transpired.

It is unclear, even now, whether Fritz Haarmann truly sold human flesh on the black market. The meat that he was selling during this period, though, was definitely prepared in the same way that he prepared the bodies of his victims. Reduced to minced meat, so that its origin could not be recognised. In those tight times, even the wealthy of Hanover with whom he did much of his business accepted the necessity of overlooking many things. If they were sold some horse meat instead of the beef that they were promised, it was a small compromise exchanged for the possibility of having no fresh meat at all. Fritz was generally considered to be reliable by his buyers, so there can be no question that the majority of the pork and beef that he sold each day were sourced from those farmers around the city who could spare it, but the exact weights he was being sold were never recorded, given the illicit nature of the business dealings. It's even possible that he was cutting his two meat sources together to disguise the unusual flavour of human flesh.

It had been some time since Fritz had thrown a bone to the local police, so he made arrangements with them to raid his new apartment in early June, once he was certain that all remnants of his victims had been thoroughly cleaned away, and those items that he truly meant to fence had been secreted elsewhere. The timing of the thing was vital, as the police did not only want to capture the stolen goods that he'd have passing through, but also the criminals that were selling them to him. Three prolific burglars had an appointment with Fritz on the day of the raid, carrying with them ample evidence of their crimes that they wanted him to sell along for them. They were all caught in the act, and they were all hauled off to the station together.

To maintain his reputation as a police informant, Fritz felt it was necessary to make grand gestures like this sometimes, but he did not care for the sacrifices involved. To prove to his usual clientele that he was not an informant and that the police were just as hard on him as anyone else, he would have to be tried and convicted for his crimes as a fence. Accordingly, in early June he was jailed for three whole weeks. It was long enough for his absence to be noted, but not so long that his business dealings might fall into disrepair. During Fritz's time imprisoned, Hans lived full-time in the apartment on Neue Straße. Not so much managing his business for him, but certainly keeping an eye on the place and ensuring that nothing too dramatic would be awaiting his partner on his return home.

On June 25th, Fritz was released, slightly ahead of schedule, due to his good behaviour and to the private confidence shared between the warden and the Hanover police about the man's value back on the street.

He showed that value almost immediately after arriving back in Hanover. Because of his early release, there was no time for Hans or his friends to organise his customary welcome home party, so he decided to make his own entertainment.

Ernst Ehrenberg was thirteen years old when Fritz saw him in the street. He was off running an errand for his parents at the time, the kind of thing that a boy that age would have been doing two or three times a day without any issue or concern. This time, he would not be returning home from running that errand. In essence, he'd be running it for the rest of his life.

With a combination of cajoling and physical force, Fritz hauled the little boy home to his apartment, slightly saddened to find that while it had been kept well, Hans was not currently around to enjoy the bounty that he had just reaped. Still, he would not let it go to waste. With the boy being so much smaller than him, Fritz didn't even have to murder him before raping him. The boy was alive, screams strangled by one strong hand around his throat, as Fritz thrust into him over and over. Blood running freely.

When Hans did return home later that evening after his dinner date, it was to an unpleasant surprise and an all too familiar smell.

Fritz was still working on the corpse when Hans walked in on him, the smaller bones and parts were more difficult to work with. The joints fiddlier work than he was accustomed to. Normally he would have had everything divided up and packaged by now. Instead, he was still slick with blood and sweat. Looming up in the dim lamp-light of the room like something out of a nightmare.

Hans managed to master himself enough to welcome his lover home, but that was as far as their conversation went. He retreated to the other room until the bloody work of corpse disposal was done, and wondered, not for the first time, just what kind of monster he had shackled himself to. It was not until he could hear Fritz's gentle snoring that he finally eased himself through to their room and settled on the far side of the bed. As far as he could get from Fritz without ending his rest on the floorboards.

In the coming month, Hans did not go out of his way to point to the boys that he wanted dead, and Fritz did not seem to have the energy to actively pursue any on his own. Though it made his skin crawl, Hans had been showing the older man more and more affection, perhaps hoping to curb the older man's desires enough that he would not have to come home to another unexpected slaughter.

For Fritz's part, his focus seemed to be mainly on getting his criminal enterprises back on track after neglecting them during his time in prison, and in the prior month as his bloodlust had overrun all common sense. He became gradually more irritable as the month stretched on, and he found no satisfaction, even when Hans willingly gave himself over to the man.

They made it into a second busy month, with Fritz running back and forth between his work and the police station almost daily, trying to stay abreast of all the crime that was happening in Hanover during the height of summer, when it seemed that despite the shorter nights, criminals were working with a kind of furious intensity.

His reputation with the police may have been secure, but that did not mean he could rest on his laurels, it was vital that he provide them with a steady flow of information, not just the occasional big bust. He intended to make himself so invaluable as an informant that they would never again look at him as a suspect, and he was succeeding.

But despite all the things that should have marked his life as a success in terms of his peers, Fritz still found himself unsatisfied. He was an outsider, even among outsiders, something different from the common criminals that he brushed elbows with every day. Something driven not by his father's desire for success and reputation above all things, but by an entirely different set of impulses.

By August, he was tired of good behaviour, tired of doing all the right things and finding no satisfaction. No matter how pliant his beloved Hans might have made himself behave, he found that there were cravings that living flesh just could not satisfy, and such release as he could find with liquor and his boy were insignificant little drips passing through cracks in the dam. He needed to relieve the pressure. He needed to be who he was.

Heinrich Strauss was an 18-year-old violin prodigy, travelling to a lesson when he went missing. The next day, Fritz was talking to smugglers about the quality of a violin that had just come into his possession. It was valuable indeed, and he was able to secure a decent price for it from one of the many pawn shops flourishing in Hanover, who then passed it out of town to be sold for an extortionate amount to a collector before anyone could make the connection with whoever it was stolen from. Fritz was left with the violin’s case, which he tossed onto the growing heap of miscellaneous knick-knacks that had been left over from his various house guests.

Paul Bronischewski was a teenage boy of Polish descent visiting his uncle in Hanover who never made it to the old man's home. He had been passing through Hanover Central train station, Fritz’s usual haunt, when he vanished. He was not well off, he had nothing of real value on his person, there was no reason for any mugger to seize him. No reason at all for him to die.

Richard Graf was new in Hanover, but he had already fallen in with the wrong crowd and was picked up by the police for sleeping rough and being inebriated in one of the city’s garden parks. He was due for release from jail the next morning and had already gone through processing when he was approached by an eccentric-looking man in plain clothes that he assumed to be a detective. After a short conversation, the stranger offered up some help, obviously feeling paternal over the teenager who was young enough to have been his own son. He explained that there were jobs available in Hanover for those willing to work and that Richard could pull himself up by his bootstraps, escaping from the downward spiral he and his friends had been on. After Richard bade farewell to his friends who would go on to continue drinking and carousing in town until they were essentially banished back home to their families, he went off with this "detective" to learn more about the opportunities that were available to upstanding and handsome young men in the city of Hanover. He was never seen again.

Wilhelm Erdner went missing from outside Hanover station in early October. The sixteen-year-old had parked his bike there while running errands about the town centre. Errands that he was never seen performing, and that he never returned from. Later that day Hans would be seen collecting the boy's bicycle from where it had been abandoned, and a few days later Fritz would post a classified advert in the local paper to sell it. When his parents enquired as to his whereabouts with the police, they mentioned a specific detective, Fritz 'Honnerbrock', who their son was well acquainted with, and who might be able to offer some insight.

Two weeks later, Hermann Wolf was reported missing by his parents. The sixteen-year-old had been out and about in Hanover, and his clothes could be seen on the backs of many of Haarmann's acquaintances, and those that they sold to. If he had been processed by the police immediately when they picked him up, they likely would have found that he vanished from their police station. That some unnamed detective had come to collect the boy from holding and walked out into the streets with him. Only the accounts of his cellmates and friends ever brought this to the police's attention, and only weeks later when he still hadn't turned up.

Three days after that disappearance, thirteen-year-old Heinz Brinkmann missed his train back to Clausthal after a day in the city, vanishing mysteriously from Hanover station, just like so many young boys had before him.

The rate of the disappearances accelerated to the point that even Hanover police could no longer ignore it. Yet they remained nothing more than missing boys during a time of massive societal and political upheaval. Runaways, job-seekers or those who had fallen in with criminals. There were so many reasons that young men were vanishing from their normal lives, not even accounting for the veritable flood of them who were heading out beyond Germany's borders to seek opportunities in places that were not being deliberately stunted by the crippling treaties that the German people had been forced to sign after their defeat in the Great War. Yet they did begin their investigation into the missing boys about that time, all the same, inquiring with their best informant to see if anyone in the criminal underworld might have had some knowledge of where they were all vanishing to. Fritz told them that he'd look into it, but mysteriously never managed to turn anything up.

Adolf Hannappel was approached by Fritz Haarmann at the Hanover train station and seen departing with the older man. He was fifteen years old at the time of his disappearance in November 1923. Looking for an apprenticeship in the city, like so many of the boys flooding into town. Conflicting reports from friends and witnesses would later paint two distinct pictures of this moment. One in which Haarmann pursued the young man exclusively because of his good looks, another in which Hans, jealous of the boy's good looks and fine clothes, had unleashed his older lover on the teenager like a tamed wolf.

Adolf Hennies was nineteen when the same thing happened to him. He had come to the city in search of work, met up with Haarmann, who proposed that he introduce him to some influential people in town who might be able to help, and then the boy fell off the map.

Despite this veritable frenzy of extra-curricular activity, Fritz did not forget about the importance of maintaining his business relationships. When one of his allies in the underworld was standing trial and he learned that the star witness, Ernst Speiker, was a handsome seventeen-year-old, he assured his friend that he would intervene and ensure that the boy never opened his mouth in the courthouse. The matter that he was testifying on was hardly life or death, the potential punishment that could have been brought down on Fritz's ally was a relative slap on the wrist. The boy's disappearance drew infinitely more attention than his testimony would have. Yet without their star witness, the trial did fall apart, leaving Fritz's criminal friend more confused than grateful.

Heinrich Koch was eighteen when he vanished, but of all the missing boys, he was probably the one that gave the police the least concern. He had long been involved in criminal activity, well-reported and represented to the police by their favourite informant, Fritz Haarmann. It was assumed that he had fled from the town to avoid attention from the police, or had been consumed by the underworld that he had played his part in. It was difficult to muster up any sympathy for him when he'd deliberately committed himself to crime from a young age and had shown every sign of proceeding into a lifetime of wickedness. The police knew that if he returned to town they would hear about it soon enough. After all, he was known to be a close acquaintance of their informant, Fritz Haarmann.

Willi Senger vanished a couple of weeks after the last known sighting of Koch. The pattern of his disappearance was barely different from previous ones, he was headed into Hanover from the suburbs with a friend, travelling by train. He was picked up from the train station and never seen again. Only the fact that his clothes had his name sewn into them indicated that he had been one of Haarmann's victims.

Herman Speichert was a fifteen-year-old electrician's apprentice doing some grunt work in the neighbourhood. His work uniform did not sell, so it would remain amidst the piles of clothes in Haarmann's warehouse apartment for many years, forgotten and buried.

Alfred Hogrefe vanished the next month, in April 1924. He was another apprentice, this time to a mechanic who reported his absence when he didn't show up for work. His clothes did sell but could all be traced back to Haarmann through his network of contacts.

Hermann Bock was last seen by his friends heading off to a dinner date with Fritz Haarmann. He had seen something of the glamorous life that Hans seemed to enjoy, and he wanted a slice of it for himself. What he received instead was a delicious meal, a delicious bottle of wine and the sensation of Fritz's teeth closing through the front of his throat when they began to kiss. The only thing that could be considered good about his death, was that he was at least in his twenties, rather than being a child, but any hope that his death might have sated Haarmann's awful hunger for violence and death would swiftly have been proven empty. Little more than a day later, Fritz was back on the hunt.

Wilhelm Apel disappeared from the police station and Robert Witzel vanished while on a night out to visit the circus, both were teenagers who Fritz had calculated would not be missed. Police reports were filed for both of their disappearances, but once more the sheer volume of people coming and going from every city during this period masked the crimes.

It was the month of May that Fritz's tastes seemed to take a turn for the darker. Heinz Martin was only fourteen when Fritz picked the apprentice locksmith up from Hanover Station with promises of a master who would treat him more kindly.

He did murder Fritz Wittig that month, on the 26th, at the behest of the jealous and avaricious Hans. Wittig was seventeen, almost a grown man working a man's job as a travelling salesman, but it seemed that whatever urge had now seized Fritz was no longer satisfied by mere murder and rape. Killing at Hans' command did not give him the sense of joy that he experienced when he picked out his victims, hunted them, and tricked them into his lair. He had to go out again after Wittig had been slaughtered and butchered to seek out his own satisfaction. Hans went out too, in his finely appointed new suit.

The way that Fritz found his satisfaction that day is still considered by many to be the evilest of his crimes. Even though he should have been exhausted and sated by his earlier murder, he took to the streets once more and came upon Friedrich Abeling. A boy of only eleven who was playing truant from school. He took him home with promises of treats and toys, he stripped him of his clothes, and he raped that child before biting out his throat. It was the most depraved of all his murders, but even that did not seem to satisfy him.

Just days after his double murder, Fritz came upon a second young man by the name of Heinrich Koch who was on his way to college. Fritz managed to convince the boy to skip class and to go out drinking and carousing with him and his friends. One thing led to another, they both ended up back at Fritz's apartment, in Fritz's bed, entangled in each other's limbs in a way that might have seemed like romance, at least until Fritz bit down.

Erich de Vries was the last known victim of this horrific spree. A seventeen-year-old boy who went missing just like all the others. There was nothing special about his death, nothing unusual about it at this point in Haarmann's life. It is only notable because it happened to coincide with Haarmann's bloody frenzy finally being brought to a halt. There was no sense that it was a maestro's final performance. Rather it was just another day's regular work for the man.

Completely forgettable.

The River of Bones

The sheer volume of bodies that Fritz was processing necessitated a more abridged version of his previous disposal methods. Where before he would have spent a day or more carefully stripping all the flesh from the bones before finding a secure place to bury them under cover of darkness, now he merely dismembered many of his victims before carting them off to unmarked graves. Even those that he did process to the full extent of his butchering skill left behind such an abundance of bones that he was forced to take shortcuts in disposing of them.

On May 17th 1924, some children playing at the edge of the river running by Herrenhausen Castle found a human skull washed up on the muddy riverbanks prompting speculation that some historic grave on the grounds had been uncovered by the recent rainfall.

On May 29th, another skull was discovered in a mill run closer to Hanover, eliminating any hopes of an archaeological discovery up by the castle, and opening the door to more morbid speculation.

On the 13th of June, two more skulls were discovered embedded in the river sediment and taken at once to the police, and from there to the pathologists of Hanover University for examination. The flesh was absent, not through decay, but through deliberate removal. And of the four skulls, most were from men in their late teens or early twenties, with only one having the appearance of a twelve-year-old's decapitated head. In all cases, blade marks on the base of the skull revealed that the head had been forcibly severed from the neck with a sharp implement.

Strangely, this quality of the bones made the police less suspicious of foul play. They had been professionally prepared, rather than simply being corpses dumped into the river, so it was assumed that these were the remains of bodies that had been worked on at the anatomical institute of Gottingen, where medical students would come to study the bodies of the dead and learn more of their workings while removing their various bodily systems in layers.

Gottingen of course denied this possibility; they were not in the habit of misplacing human remains, whether whole or broken down to mere skulls. Yet the police suspected that this was dissembling to cover up some error on their part rather than the full truth of the matter.

Still, they couldn't publicly accuse such an institute of outright lying, so various other theories were circulated around the station. There has been an outbreak of typhoid in the town of Alfield, upriver, that some proposed may have been the cause. Grave robbers were the favourite scapegoat of the police. The majority of the police involved in the investigation did not have the medical knowledge necessary to grasp what the pathologists had told them. When they saw a skull, they associated it with a long-dead body, and there had been a spate of grave robberies not so long ago in Hanover. It would have been quite possible that body thieves carrying their ill-gotten gains off to sell to somewhere like Gottingen had been startled by a patrol and dumped their corpses off the side of a bridge. It was a neat little explanation that still put some of the blame on the institute in Gottingen without the requirement for any direct challenge to their esteemed position. The fact that the evidence didn't point to this scenario in any way was mere happenstance.

Though they attempted to circulate this rumour and quiet the rumble of public alarm, the papers began reporting on the skulls having been found and the low-scale panic soon kicked into a frenzy when some children playing out in the marshland near the town of Döhren discovered a burlap sack full of human bones of all shapes and sizes.

The rumour mill began to run out of control, and for the first time, the newspapers began to take an interest in all the missing teenage boys in Hanover, demanding information and reports from the police that the police were extremely reluctant to hand over, given how damning it looked for them. They managed to pawn off the previous year's records of missing boys to the papers as though they were the only ones that had been collated, not even realising that those numbers were more than damning enough. Six hundred missing boys in the city of Hanover. Six hundred.

The police had discounted a great many of these as runaways, or poorly reported migration out of the city caused by the chaos and upheaval in the aftermath of the war, and they were quite right to do so, as history would eventually prove that many of these missing person reports were entirely erroneous. However, the fact of the matter was that even accounting for those things the sheer volume of missing teenagers was shocking.

The papers' investigation found that almost all of those missing were between fourteen and eighteen years of age. A very clear cut-off that would not be explained by natural migration or runaways. The rumour mill began spinning to life, with talk of a murderer of boys soon mutating into talks of a man-eater. A cannibal killer who had turned to the butchery of his fellow man during the hard times following the war. Some of the less reputable papers had begun their own 'investigations' into the quality of meat being sold on the black market, which was soon tied into this story with the strong implication that the missing boys had ended up on someone's dinner plate.

Such a thought was sufficient to drive the entire city and all of its surrounding area into an absolute frenzy. Communities began to pull together around the families of the missing, and on the next high holy day when everyone was off work – Whit Sunday – a massive mob of hundreds of citizens spread out from the city, searching through all of the Old Town, the small paths and bridges around the river and out into the countryside in search of human remains. The vastness of the undertaking was unprecedented in German history, and all spurred on by thoughts of a bogeyman stealing the youth of the city. A multitude of bones was discovered in that crusade, so many that the police's ability to assess them and cobble them together into full bodies was compromised by the sheer volume. University students and the whole of the Gottingen institute offered up their services to help work through all of the bodies that had been discovered and try to help identify the remains through science.

Some portion of them could be accounted for by animal carcasses, others were so old that they were likely remnants from one of the many wars that had been waged on German soil throughout its history, but enough were found that were fresh and new, particularly in the areas around the Leine river, that the police were spurred on into further action.

Working with the city's municipal workers, they set to work on a grand undertaking, damming the river before it came into the city and forcing the water level to drop sufficiently so that the riverbed could be explored.

It took only moments before the first team turned up bones. They were bagged up and taken off to be studied. No sooner were they removed from the river than another set was found, then another, and another. Over the course of a day, teams walked the length of the river that normally ran through Hanover, and that day they found over five hundred different clusters of bones, some that had been eroded for months by the river waters, some that were fresh enough that every knife mark on the joints where they had been separated was still visible. After the diligent work of all the city's mortuaries, medical institutes and medical students twenty-two distinct bodies were re-assembled. The remainder of the bones that had been discovered could have made up anywhere from an additional dozen to a hundred bodies but were so incomplete and broken down that it was impossible to reconstruct them sufficiently for anyone to know for certain.

The mass murders had now garnered national, and indeed, international attention. The 'Werewolf of Hanover' had become a horror story that had captured the imagination of readers and reporters around the world. With this attention, it had ceased to be a failure of parochial investigation and instead became a matter of importance to the state. An embarrassment to the fledgling nation of Weimar Germany, and evidence to those who looked down upon the German people that they were all savages dressed in the clothes of civilisation. The matter had to be resolved, and swiftly, so detectives from Berlin were dispatched to take over the investigation.

Usually, this sort of intervention causes a massive impediment to any investigation as those assigned are those who are in political favour rather than those who are the most competent, and there is a great deal of friction relating to jurisdictional clashes. However, it seems that an outsider's perspective was precisely what was required to bring the killer of boys to justice.

For several weeks, these detectives pored over all of the information that was available to them, examining all of the case files for the missing boys, poring over the witness testimonies and drawing their conclusions without familiarity masking anybody's true intentions. Meanwhile, every single known sex criminal and thief in the whole of Hanover was pulled in for interviews with the police, to account for their movements over the past months, particularly concerning the dates on which the missing boys who had been identified from their bones had last been seen.

Almost immediately one name jumped out from the various accounts. Fritz Haarmann. He was known to be a dealer in black market meat and clothing, openly homosexual with a criminal history of sexually assaulting teenaged boys, and he was well known among those that were interviewed in the intervening weeks as offering shelter to every runaway boy that he came across.

The Berlin detectives could not grasp why the man wasn't already in a jail cell facing questioning until they spoke to their colleagues from Hanover and heard all the myriad excuses that they made for Fritz. He was on their team. He had taken the fall, time and again, to help them get real dangerous criminals off the streets. The information that he provided had proved fundamental in hundreds of investigations. Then there were the more hushed rumours, the ones which indicated that junior officers had been informed that Haarmann was off limits because he provided the station's upper echelons with the meat they needed to put on their tables. That he was in bed with the criminal investigation department which squashed any case that the state tried to raise against him. Beyond that, there were the personal accounts of the police who dealt with him, who found the idea that the funny little effeminate man could be a danger to absolutely anyone laughable. To them, he was a joke, a harmless expression of what homosexuality would be if it were legalized, who was doing nobody any harm and helping Hanover as much as he could from his rather tenuous position on the lowest rung of the social ladder.

The Berlin detectives looked at him through an entirely different lens. Here was a known sexual predator who targeted victims like their missing people. Someone who had a reputation around town for taking in youths like these missing people under the guise of pseudo-parental concern, and then initiating them into a world of debauchery that most never escaped. He was known to live close to the Hanover station where the majority of the known victims had originally been abducted, and to frequent the station as a result of his information-gathering work for the local police. The only thing that was missing was a signed confession.

They set out to find Fritz immediately, heading directly to his well-known address and discovering the door locked and nobody present. An officer was stationed there to keep watch while the detectives moved on to hunt through Haarmann's usual haunts. It would not take them long to locate him.

Their first port of call was the Hanover Central Train Station where he had done so much of his hunting, and as they moved slowly through the building, searching all the quiet nooks and crannies hidden about the place, they heard the sound of a struggle.

Irritated to have their hunt interrupted by some petty crime, the detectives nonetheless moved to intervene in whatever squabble was unfolding, only to discover that in the deep shadows a teenager was being pinned against the wall by a grown man. His hands thrust down the front of the boy's trousers and his lips on the boy's neck. They hauled the perpetrator off the child and were all set to begin beating him when they realised that it was Fritz Haarmann himself. Caught in the act.

The boy ran for it before he could be dragged along to recount his trauma and bear witness, but the detectives had no concerns about their arrest being considered lawful with the sheer number of officers on site bearing witness to the sordid state of affairs.

He was flung immediately into a cell at the police station where until now he'd had free reign to wander. The cell was locked and the local police were forbidden to communicate with him in any way. Then the Berlin detectives took the house key from the man and headed off to his apartment.

What they found would haunt them for the rest of their lives.

The apartment reeked like a slaughterhouse, there were bloodstains, not only on the butchers' tools that Fritz had left lying out, but everywhere. There were arterial sprays on the walls, blood soaked into the mattress. Almost every room showed signs that death had occurred there.

Bones and meat were absent from the rooms, but there was so much other evidence stockpiled there that an actual body might have been superfluous. Every room of the converted space was occupied with piles of clothing and stolen belongings. Some of it could be accounted for by the crimes of others, and Fritz's role as a fence, but unless there were burglars out in Hanover specifically breaking into the homes of teenage boys and making off with a single outfit of their clothing before attempting to fence those clothes through Haarmann, the idea that the majority of what was stowed in his home could be a result of that illicit business rather than a campaign of murder and theft was unconscionable.

Later study proved that the bloodstains around the house were human, and from multiple different sources. The science of blood splatter analysis was in its early infancy at the time, but many of the investigators had fought in the Great War and seen death first-hand often enough to bc able to parse the meanings of the rusty paintings across every surface in Fritz's home.

As the detectives began cataloguing their findings, Hans returned home. At first, he believed that this was one of Fritz's usual scheduled raids, and dawdled right inside, greeting the officers in attendance like they were old friends, but in moments he was clapped in handcuffs and led out before he could interfere in the investigation further. He was charged as an accomplice to Haarmann's crimes, without fully explaining to him what those were, so he went along quietly, expecting that he'd find himself released as soon as Fritz had finished filling out paperwork.

Piece by piece, the local police and the detectives from Berlin began to work their way through the vast heaps of clothing and personal belongings that filled Fritz Haarmann's humble abode. His dining table became the centre of the investigation, with individual items being paired with others to slowly reconstruct the outfits that missing boys were known to have been wearing and carrying. From the hat of one boy to the violin case of another. All the little fragments of their last day on earth, pushed back together like pieces of a jigsaw just long enough to incriminate their killer.

From what was found, and from their own files, they managed to put together a dossier connecting Fritz Haarmann to twenty-seven distinct victims. These were the ones that he would be charged with killing, but with mounting horror, the investigators looked back upon the rest of the rooms and realised how much they had not managed to connect. The clothing and stolen items that could not be connected to Fritz's business as a fence and could not be connected with the twenty-seven victims that they planned to charge him for killing accounted for seventy-five per cent of the contents of the room. The actual death toll of Haarmann's frenzied slaughter of the city's boys could have been over one hundred. Or higher still. Many of the items that he had acquired from early victims had been sold along. Even pieces of clothing from the latest of the dead had already been worn by others. It would take weeks, if not months to track down many of those sold items and tie them back to Haarmann, but now that he was in captivity, they had the time to do so.

In one of the interrogation cells of Hanover Police Station, Fritz sat at a table, trying his best to stay still. It seemed that nerves were getting the better of him. He wiggled in his seat, constantly. He licked his lips over and over until spittle was dribbling down onto his chin. His hands were in constant motion, preening at himself. Smoothing his clothes, fidgeting with his hair, rubbing over his fingernails to ensure that they were smooth. Just a day before, this place would have held no fear for him. He had power over it, and over everyone within it. But now that the detectives from Berlin had arrived, everything was changing. There were no smiles and nods from the detectives. There wasn't even the annoyance that he saw when they brought him in on some petty charge and he had to weasel his way out of it. They wouldn't look at him at all.

The silence, more than anything else, had told him that he was in serious trouble this time. By now one of his buddies on the force would usually have dropped in to chew him out about getting handsy with the kid at the train station. They might have even knocked him around a bit, and he'd take it because he deserved it for getting caught with his hand in the cookie jar. But instead, they'd put him in here and said nothing. He didn't even know what he was being charged with yet.

He smoked his cigars, and he waited. One, then another, then another burned down to nothing but embers. Finally, he lost his patience and banged on the cell door, but still, nobody came to tell him off and send him on his way. This must have been their latest scare tactic, to get him back on the straight and narrow. That's what this must all have been about, they knew that the usual slap on the wrist wasn't working so they wanted to put the wind up him. They had no idea who they were dealing with, none of them ever did. The only one who knew him for what he really was had to be his sweet boy Hans, and he knew that kid's lips were forever going to be sealed. Hans had benefitted from Fritz's largesse for years, and betrayal would have tarred him with the same brush of guilt as Fritz himself. The boy strode around wearing Fritz's victims' clothes a day after pointing them out to him and whispering in his ear. He didn't have the cops on his side, he'd be the one to be locked away forever if the murders ever came out. Not Fritz, he was still in control. He didn't need to be worrying. The police knew him. They loved him. He fed them. He made their jobs easier. He was in control. He was always in control.

When the detectives from Berlin came in to interrogate him, he leaned forward in his chair trying to catch the eye of one of his friends on the force, trying to let them know he was here, that some strangers in town had arrested him by accident. None would meet his eye.

It took him a moment to tune in to what these Berliners were saying to him, he didn't recognise any of the names that they were saying, and he didn't understand what any of it had to do with him. It was only when the pictures of the boys, his beautiful boys, were laid out before him that he began to understand the depth of the trouble that he was in.

He hadn't prepared for this. Despite all the careful calculation that he usually put into his crimes, he never thought about what he would do if he were caught for this particular crime. Probably because he knew, ultimately that there was nothing to plan for. There was no defence that he could muster. There was no lie that he could tell that might excuse him. If he was caught for this, then it was the end. The end of everything.

He asked for a cup of coffee, and for a fresh pack of cigars, which the interviewing officers were reluctant to give him until he explained that he'd show them where to find the bones of Erich de Vries once they were done talking.

What followed was a garbled mess of confession, lies and omissions that may have been deliberate, or may have been entirely accidental. In truth, Fritz did not have a clear memory of every victim that he had killed, or the when and where of his encounters with them. Part of that was due to the hazy pseudo-orgasmic state he was in during most of the murders, and part of it was no doubt due to the sheer volume of killing that he had done, they had all begun to bleed into one another.

In another room of the station, Hans had flipped on Fritz almost immediately, giving the police details of every crime that he was aware of and listing off the times and dates that his wardrobe had been filled out. He claimed to have been coerced and tormented by Fritz, rather than being a willing participant in their relationship, insisted upon his own heterosexuality and did all that he could to make it clear that he was a victim in all of this. One who had suffered at least as badly as the other boys that had died, possibly more so since they at least had the escape of death while Hans was not even allowed that release.

When this was explained to Fritz, his story changed once more. Here he was, an effeminate joke of a man, how could he possibly have been responsible for all these awful things when he was such a silly character? Hans was the mastermind behind it all, and he was tired of covering up for him. Ever since they'd met, Hans had bullied and belittled him, any of their friends could tell the police that it was true. He had been nothing more than a meal ticket for the boy, and even though Fritz had tried to keep him on the path of the straight and narrow, he had instead dragged Fritz down into the pits of depravity.

The police, understandably, now that they had received some fragments of his confession, were dubious as to the veracity of this newly spun tale. Particularly given how few of their witness accounts tied Hans to the scene of any crime and how every one of them placed Fritz firmly there.

In the end, the truth was assumed to lie somewhere between the two extremes of the criminals' testimonies. That both men bore some guilt for their involvement in the murders, but that the burden of it primarily fell on Fritz's shoulders. Something that seemed quite obvious once he got into discussing the breaking down of the bodies, supposedly at young Hans' behest.

Despite the long list of murdered boys already tied to Fritz, what remained in his apartment after all the evidence was gathered was a testament to a far darker world than anyone was willing to admit that they lived in. In total, only around one-quarter of all the boy's clothes found in the building was accounted for by the known victims and the other crimes that Fritz was serving as a fence for. Three-quarters of that vast hoard had come from unknown victims. If the amount of found goods matched the accounting for the twenty-seven young men and boys that the police had a solid enough case to pursue then the count of victims had to be in excess of one hundred.

The press ran wild now that an arrest had been made, Fritz's picture was taken as frequently as it was possible for it to be taken in the brief moments he was being moved between cell and courthouse and appeared on front pages across Europe. There was no language at the time to discuss the type of criminal that Fritz was, so they called him a wolf-man, a vampire, anything at all that might distance him from the unfortunate truth that he was just a man, like any other, and that any man might be capable of crimes such as his. His image became ingrained in the public consciousness as the face of evil, completely at odds with everything that people thought they knew of murderers. This was no low-born thug, he looked more like a dandy. Like the homosexual that everyone knew in their town, who was harmless, if still to be looked down on as a degenerate.

Trials and Tribulation

The trial began on the fourth of December 1924, expedited greatly by the public fervour surrounding the matter. The police had little time to build a case given the sheer volume of crimes that were involved, but with Fritz having delivered them at least one set of bones, his confused confessions were being taken as truth and would serve as sufficient rope to hang him with.

Perversely, now that he no longer felt any need to hide his true nature, Fritz Haarmann basked in his newfound celebrity. He minced into court with no attempt at masculinity but balanced such displays with such coarseness that the Judge was often appalled enough at his behaviour to bring proceedings to a halt. He smoked his rough cigars incessantly throughout proceedings, shouting up to the people observing, shouting to the press who waited with bated breath for his latest outburst so they could dutifully quote every scandalous word.

For the first time, in the courthouse, Fritz came face to face with the families of those that he had killed. Each of them an aching emotional wound that he delighted in pouring more salt into. He had no contrition, no sympathy for them whatsoever, implying that most of the boys he'd abducted and slaughtered had been begging for his carnal attentions and that they deserved all that had come to them as a result of their wantonness. One by one, the charges were brought before the court. A picture of each victim was presented to the jury, and then the gruesome tale of what Fritz had done to each of them was recounted. Two, he blamed entirely upon young Hans, who was being tried separately in another courtroom, but the rest he seemed almost delighted to accept responsibility for.

One young man's photograph was passed to him in court, and Fritz announced immediately that he had not killed him. Given his acceptance of every charge up until now, this understandably caused some confusion among both the beleaguered defence lawyer and the prosecution, not to mention the family of the dead boy. It was only after the chaos had died down a little that Fritz could explain himself. The boy was not nearly handsome enough for him to have picked him out. He explained to the family that their dead son was simply too ugly for him to have murdered him. There was no attraction, so there would have been no murder. He wouldn't have killed their son without raping him, and he certainly wouldn't have given that hideous face the time of day.

Chaos and screaming erupted in court while Fritz sat back, with a big grin on his face, puffing away on his cigar. It was only when the prosecution presented all of the evidence that Fritz had indeed killed the boy, and still had the victim's personal effects in his possession at the time of his arrest that he conceded that he must have killed him then, wondering aloud if perhaps he had been drunk when picking out his victim for that day.

There were other pictures presented to him that he claimed to have no memory of after that point, but he would announce 'charge it to my account' or 'I assume he's one of mine.'

When pressed on his motives, and premeditation of his crimes, Fritz was dismissive. He claimed that he did not know why he had killed, even though in retrospect at least some part of it had clearly been calculated, there was also some part that was the result of a murderous drive that even now, with all his horrors on display, he did not dare speak of. Psychological evaluation before the trial had ascertained that Fritz was responsible for his actions but had not pried any more deeply into his psyche than that. Primarily because any attempts to dig in any deeper were met with deliberate attempts at subterfuge and diversion. One analysis would return a diagnosis, while the other a completely antithetical one. It became clear to them early on that he was playing games with them, using his past knowledge of psychiatric care to befuddle their results.

Numerous exhibits were brought before the court, including the many skeletal remains that had been retrieved from the river and elsewhere, and once more, while Fritz was happy to lay claim to them as his victims, he nonetheless insisted on throwing a spanner into the works by claiming that the skulls must have been mismatched to bodies. He claimed that in the case of all his true victims, he had disposed of the skull by smashing it into pieces. Thus, all of these skulls must have been procured from elsewhere and stuck on for the sake of the families.

Similarly, the butcher's tools, cot bed and bucket that he had used to dispose of his victims were brought forth, but he had no clever commentary attached to these, except to say that although he may have consumed some small part of the dead by accident while causing them to be so, he had never knowingly sold any of the butchered meat that he procured from their corpses to the people of Hanover. It was another odd inconsistency in his tale; given that he'd seemed so intent upon causing the maximum amount of dismay and horror among his audience. Claiming that he'd made cannibals of half the homes of Hanover would have served that purpose well, so even if it weren't true, surely, he would have claimed it.

In truth, there is no way to know with certainty whether he butchered and sold the meat of his victims. Sufficient evidence from the time seems to point towards it. But of course, there were no official records of the black-market trade in meat that could have settled the matter.

A medical expert did testify that none of the meat found in Haarmann's apartment at the time of his arrest was human, but that did not mean that whatever he had procured from his latest victim had not already been sold along. There was ample evidence of the butchery of human flesh of course, but little more.

Testimony was supplied to show that he had been passing it off as pork, of course. Haarmann's landlady talked about the boiling of meat going on at all hours, from which Fritz would skim the fat and bottle it for sale. On a separate occasion, she told the court that her family had become ill after eating sausages that Haarmann had procured for them and encased in what he claimed were sheep intestines.

Another neighbour spoke of how often they saw Fritz departing from his apartment carrying packaged meat for sale, yet never saw him bringing deliveries in.

Other neighbours spoke of the sacks of bones that they did see departing the apartment in Fritz's company each day, that they had put down to his work, and which now seemed infinitely more sinister.

Yet another neighbour was quick to testify about all of the young men that they saw coming into Haarmann's apartment at all times of the night and day, but never saw again. When pressed on why they had not reported this irregularity to the authorities, they claimed that they believed Fritz had been selling the boys along to the foreign legion as new recruits in exchange for a stipend. It would explain why he was always flush with cash despite holding down no job.

Two of Hans' lady friends spoke about the time that they had been visiting, and on stepping into the kitchen saw what they thought was a human mouth boiling in a soup kettle. Fritz had told them it was a pig's snout, but neither had been entirely convinced and had refused to visit again. One had even reported the incident to the police, who eerily replied in exactly the same manner, regarding pig snouts.

This, and further testimony from those who had reported Haarmann's behaviour through the years, began to paint a very grim picture of the Hanover police department. A picture made all the worse by the addition that he had only been brought to justice when policemen from Berlin had been the ones to come in and almost immediately solve the case. There had been dozens if not hundreds of complaints through the years about Fritz's behaviour, and they had all been ignored because he was in the favour of the local police. Even outright crimes that had been witnessed were not prosecuted because of the possibility of an immediate cessation of information being fed to the police by their favourite informant.

These were meant to be the people standing between the victims of the world and their would-be killers, and the mounting evidence that they had essentially aided and abetted the murderer in his works was as much of a horror as the crimes themselves. Hanover's police would have been the laughingstock of the continent if it were not for the absolute disdain that everyone now held for them.

When finally called to the stand, Haarmann's testimony was, quite predictably, nothing short of a circus. He had made a mockery of proceedings from the very beginning and had no intention of stopping now. He told some part of the tale of his life. He explained how he had tried his best to fit into society's standards but found that they were in direct opposition to his fundamental nature. He explained that he had done what he could to do some good with the position in which he found himself and that he had done all he could within the realms of the law to support himself before, having no viable alternative, being forced to turn to crime. He offered a lot of talk but nothing substantial beyond a rambling diatribe against the nation that he felt had betrayed him time and time again. His lawyer had pointed out that the evidence against him in the case of many of the murders was entirely circumstantial early in the proceedings. As a trader in stolen goods, it was entirely feasible that the victims' clothes had found their way into Fritz's possession by illegitimate means for black market resale but that the simple possession of these clothes could, in no way, be construed as actual proof of a murderous disposition. He'd killed them, some at the behest of his betrayer and lover Grans, some for no reason at all that he could think of.

Yet while this seemed to be as idiotic and insane a stance as any had ever taken on the stand, close observers couldn't help but note that there was still a note of calculation in his words. He was reciting his rambling as though from a script, as though he had planned it all out in advance, and he looked ever more irritated each time that he was interrupted by one counsel or the other.

He was freely confessing to the crimes of which he was accused, that the police had presented evidence for, yet all of the other crimes that the accrued piles of goods in his home spoke to went unmentioned. He did not incriminate himself further than he felt he had already been incriminated, and he did not let anything slip that might have given the state a stronger case against him than it already had. Even in his supposed madness, he was conniving and plotting for his maximum advantage.

On the 19th of December, he was acquitted of several of his crimes due to insufficient evidence presented by the prosecution, and the circumstantial nature of what was presented. Similarly, some of the blame for the three murders was considered to be shared with his young accomplice and confidante, still undergoing his own trial in another chamber. Yet for the vast majority of his crimes, he bore the full weight of punishment that the court could hand down. It was inevitable, given the public attention in the case, and the universal condemnation of his crimes. He would face death for his crimes, and many felt that he was getting off very lightly at that. He made a final statement after the judge had handed down his sentence, and all of the quips and monstrosity of his prior performances seemed to come apart in an instant. 'Condemn me to death. I ask only for justice.

I am not mad. Make it short; make it soon. Deliver me from this life, which is a torment. I will not petition for mercy, nor will I appeal. I want to pass just one more merry night in my cell, with coffee, cheese and cigars, after which I will curse my father and go to my execution as if it were a wedding.'

He was under armed guard as he was taken from the courthouse, more for his own protection than from any risk of him escaping. What point would there have been in escaping? When his was the best-known face in all of Europe.

Hans Grans received his own death sentence for his involvement in the crimes shortly afterwards. He did not take the news with the same composure as his lover. He howled and wailed, had to be practically carried out of the room after he'd heard that he was to die. He was convicted as the accessory to two of the murders, but the thing that sealed his fate was his direct involvement in one of the murders, with witnesses having seen him literally pointing out the victim to Fritz.

Fritz made no attempt to appeal his conviction, although his lawyer did go through the motions, throwing every excuse that it was possible to come up with for why he should not be executed. The higher courts of the land were forced to give up a few of the convictions on the basis of the circumstantial evidence, but enough stuck that Fritz was still going to face the executioner when the time came.

With that done, he took it upon himself, at last, to intervene on Hans Grans' behalf. Sending a letter to the court claiming full accountability for the crimes of which Hans was accused and explaining that he was a young man who had fallen under the influence of an older and far more wicked one. He should not have been held accountable for the things that he had said and done while under duress and danger of death, any more than any man should be. It was a strangely noble act at the end of a very ignoble life. Although the nobility of it was somewhat tarnished by the fact that he'd waited until he was sure that he couldn't weasel out of his death sentence.

The court did accept Fritz's letter as fact, and Hans' sentence was commuted to merely a prison sentence of ten years. The young pimp understood very little of what had happened, or why Fritz would have come to his rescue like he did after he had done his damnedest to throw him under the bus. Perhaps, after all his time, it was true love. Or at least the closest to it that either of the men had ever known. Neither of them were saints, by any stretch of the imagination, but it seemed at least the affection that Fritz felt for his young lover was real.

From this point on, their paths diverged. Hans went to prison and suffered through twelve years of hard labour. At the end of that period, the world had changed drastically, and while he should have known freedom, he was instead taken to Sachsenhausen concentration camp where he remained until the end of the second world war. In the aftermath of that, any bad reputation that might have still clung to him had been entirely forgotten. Almost twenty years since he had been involved with Haarmann, he was just another victim of the Nazi regime, and he was able to fade into the background of history until his death in 1980.

His part in the story ended with that final letter from Haarmann to the court. The two men never saw one another again.

To await the delivery of his sentence, Fritz was taken to Hanover prison, and per German tradition, the actual date of his execution was withheld from him until the night before it was to be enacted, with the intention that it would reduce the suffering of the convicted. He was subdued throughout his incarceration, up until the final night of April 14th, 1925, when he was informed of what the morning would bring.

The chaplain of the prison was brought, and Fritz made such contrition as he could manage, trying to make his peace with God, then he retired to his cell, taking no food, as his stomach would not hold it, but instead drinking fine Brazilian coffee, of the sort that he loved best, and smoking the terrible black cigars he had always smoked.

Come dawn, he was taken outside into the yard where a guillotine had been set up. He was pale and shaking but maintained the same sense of bravado that had carried him through so much before. He seemed quite stricken at the sight of the apparatus but still managed to walk up on his own, without assistance, even turning it down when it was offered. 'I am guilty, gentlemen, but, hard though it may be, I want to die as a man.'

He knelt before the machine and placed his head in, allowing the executioner to close the lock over him. He looked out at the gathered crowd and called out. 'I repent, but I do not fear death.'

The blade came down a moment later.

With him dead, the papers were able to rehash all the gruesome details of the case again. Cementing in everyone's minds just how monstrous a man he was for all of eternity.

In the aftermath of his death, his head was taken from his remains to be examined by medical science. The actual structures of the brain were found to be perfectly normal, but there was evidence in the tissue that suggested that he had suffered from meningitis at some point in his life. Something that likely caused many of the bouts of fainting and paralysis at various points throughout his life. It did not explain his behaviour in any way, nor would any study of his brain undertaken in the years since. The whole head was preserved in formaldehyde for future researchers, but to no avail. It remained with the Göttingen medical school until 2014 when it was finally destroyed by cremation. The rest of his body was consigned to a pauper's grave, the exact location unknown. Though he had requested that a stone be erected in his memory listing him proudly as a mass murderer, the court was not willing to grant this concession.

By comparison, his victims were given a memorial. However, if people had known what lay beneath the surface of the earth then they may not have been so pleased at the sight of the triptych stone. All of the bones that had been gathered in the investigation were mixed together in a mass grave beneath the earth's surface. Too difficult to separate even when they were being laid to rest.

The image of Fritz Haarmann was seared into the mind of the public consciousness.

Homosexuality was still illegal in Germany and most of the world at this point in history, but it was typically unprosecuted because public opinion had begun to shift in favour of magnanimity. Particularly in socially progressive Weimar Germany, where people were actually beginning to live openly in homosexual relationships. The cabarets, centres of entertainment, were almost exclusively run by homosexuals, and science had begun to take a great interest in the matter of human sexuality, with many of the leading minds in the field being based in Berlin, Germany.

With the arrest of Fritz Haarmann and the awful facts of his case being brought to light, the opinions of the public were irrevocably changed. Every homosexual in Germany was tarred with the same brush. Tolerance, such as had been extended, was snatched back. In every town where people had been living openly, they now had to retreat into the shadows once more or risk outright violence as the view of them changed from that of slightly comical figures on the periphery of acceptable society to potential child murderers. It was the oldest slur on their character to have ever been spoken, now given fresh breath by a heinous crime publicised around the world.

This change in opinion fed into a rising tide of public opinion that was anything but liberal.

The most famous pictures of Nazi book burnings to have ever circulated were taken outside of the Institute of Sex Research in Berlin. When all of the research into homosexuality, intersex and transgender people was pulled from their libraries and set alight. While the rise of the Nazis was brought about by many different things, and ostensibly they railed against communism and the Jewish people that they blamed for it, it is important to remember that when the time came for them to take their first actions, before they had fully cemented their control, they chose an easy target. One that the public would not object to them sacrificing.

It is true that even if homosexuals and other "degenerates" had not been transformed into that acceptable victim then the Nazis would doubtless have found some other minority group to target first before moving on to them, but that may have taken time. It may have slowed their rise and allowed other factors to intervene. In his small way, Fritz Haarmann was responsible for the rise of Fascism in Germany and everything that later entailed.

On a personal level, Fritz Haarmann was a monster, but the evil that he did was far-reaching, even by the standards of modern-day serial killers. His actions still echoing down through history in a way that few modern-day monsters could manage.

Want More?

Did you enjoy *Butcher, Biter, Spy* and want some more True Crime?

YOUR FREE BOOK IS WAITING

From bestselling author Ryan Green

There is a man who is officially classed as "**Britain's most dangerous prisoner**"

The man's name is Robert Maudsley, and his crimes earned him the nickname "**Hannibal the Cannibal**"

This free book is an exploration of his story...

amazonkindle nook kobo iBooks

"Ryan brings the horrifying details to life. I can't wait to read more by this author!"

Get a free copy of ***Robert Maudsley: Hannibal the Cannibal*** when you sign up to join my Reader's Group.

www.ryangreenbooks.com/free-book

Every Review Helps

If you enjoyed the book and have a moment to spare, I would really appreciate a short review on Amazon. Your help in spreading the word is gratefully received and reviews make a huge difference to helping new readers find me. Without reviewers, us self-published authors would have a hard time!

Type in your link below to be taken straight to my book review page.

US	geni.us/bbsUS
UK	geni.us/bbsUK
Australia	geni.us/bbsAUS
Canada	geni.us/bbsCA

Thank you! I can't wait to read your thoughts.

About Ryan Green

Ryan Green is a true crime author who lives in Herefordshire, England with his wife, three children, and two dogs. Outside of writing and spending time with his family, Ryan enjoys walking, reading and windsurfing.

Ryan is fascinated with History, Psychology and True Crime. In 2015, he finally started researching and writing his own work and at the end of the year, he released his first book on Britain's most notorious serial killer, Harold Shipman.

He has since written several books on lesser-known subjects, and taken the unique approach of writing from the killer's perspective. He narrates some of the most chilling scenes you'll encounter in the True Crime genre.

You can sign up to Ryan's newsletter to receive a free book, updates, and the latest releases at:

WWW.RYANGREENBOOKS.COM

More Books by Ryan Green

In July 1965, teenagers Sylvia and Jenny Likens were left in the temporary care of Gertrude Baniszewski, a middle-aged single mother and her seven children.

The Baniszewski household was overrun with children. There were few rules and ample freedom. Sadly, the environment created a dangerous hierarchy of social Darwinism where the strong preyed on the weak.

What transpired in the following three months was both riveting and chilling. The case shocked the entire nation and would later be described as "The single worst crime perpetuated against an individual in Indiana's history".

More Books by Ryan Green

On 29th February 2000, John Price took out a restraining order against his girlfriend, Katherine Knight. Later that day, he told his co-workers that she had stabbed him and if he were ever to go missing, it was because Knight had killed him.

The next day, Price didn't show up for work.

A co-worker was sent to check on him. They found a bloody handprint by the front door and they immediately contacted the police. The local police force was not prepared for the chilling scene they were about to encounter.

Price's body was found in a chair, legs crossed, with a bottle of lemonade under his arm. He'd been decapitated and skinned. The "skin-suit" was hanging from a meat hook in the living room and his head was found in the kitchen, in a pot of vegetables that was still warm. There were two plates on the dining table, each had the name of one of Price's children on it.

She was attempting to serve his body parts to his children.

More Books by Ryan Green

In 1902, at the age of 11, Carl Panzram broke into a neighbour's home and stole some apples, a pie, and a revolver. As a frequent troublemaker, the court decided to make an example of him and placed him into the care of the Minnesota State Reform School. During his two-year detention, Carl was repeatedly beaten, tortured, humiliated and raped by the school staff.

At 15-years old, Carl enlisted in the army by lying about his age but his career was short-lived. He was dishonourably discharged for stealing army supplies and was sent to military prison. The brutal prison system sculpted Carl into the man that he would remain for the rest of his life. He hated the whole of mankind and wanted revenge.

When Carl left prison in 1910, he set out to rob, burn, rape and kill as many people as he could, for as long as he could. His campaign of terror could finally begin and nothing could stand in his way.

More Books by Ryan Green

In 1861, the police of a rural French village tore their way into the woodside home of Martin Dumollard. Inside, they found chaos. Paths had been carved through mounds of bloodstained clothing, reaching as high as the ceiling in some places.

The officers assumed that the mysterious maid-robber had killed one woman but failed in his other attempts. Yet, it was becoming sickeningly clear that there was a vast gulf between the crimes they were aware of and the ones that had truly been committed.

Would Dumollard's wife expose his dark secret or was she inextricably linked to the atrocities? Whatever the circumstances, everyone was desperate to discover whether the bloody garments belonged to some of the 648 missing women.

Free True Crime Audiobook

Sign up to Audible and use your free credit to download this collection of twelve books. If you cancel within 30 days, there's no charge!

WWW.RYANGREENBOOKS.COM/FREE-AUDIOBOOK

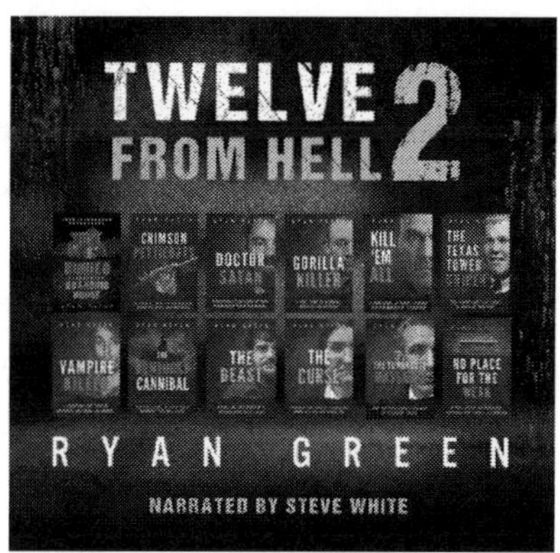

"Ryan Green has produced another excellent book and belongs at the top with true crime writers such as M. William Phelps, Gregg Olsen and Ann Rule" –**B.S. Reid**

"Wow! Chilling, shocking and totally riveting! I'm not going to sleep well after listening to this but the narration was fantastic. Crazy story but highly recommend for any true crime lover!" –**Mandy**

"Torture Mom by Ryan Green left me pretty speechless. The fact that it's a true story is just...wow" –**JStep**

"Graphic, upsetting, but superbly read and written" –**Ray C**

WWW.RYANGREENBOOKS.COM/FREE-AUDIOBOOK

Printed in Great Britain
by Amazon

e4359db8-ba22-45b7-aa82-136370d95b34R01